GCSE
POETRY
SKILLS

Andy Mort
Series Editor: Imelda Pilgrim

Nelson Thornes

Contents

Section A · Reading poetry

Section B · Exam practice

Poetry skills for GCSE

About your course

This book has been written to guide you through elements of your GCSE English Literature course. It will help you to develop skills you need to succeed, not only in your exams and assessments, but in whatever you decide to do afterwards.

New exam specifications have been introduced for students beginning English GCSE courses from September 2010 onwards. One of the main differences between the old specifications and the new is that coursework has been replaced by Controlled Assessment, and writing about poetry in Controlled Assessment conditions is an option that teachers may be able to choose if your school is following the course of a particular examination board.

Generally speaking, however, it is a requirement that all GCSE students are tested in exam conditions on their ability to write about a poem (or poems) that their teachers have *not* prepared with them as set texts. This might seem very challenging to you as a student, but a lot of teachers welcome this development, because practice for this section of the exam will enable you to develop reading skills that will make you a more independent learner. This can help raise your levels of achievement in other areas of English Language and English Literature – and in other areas of the curriculum.

Most specifically, it will support your study of set poems in other sections of the Literature exam, and also in other areas of the course, which you might not think so obviously connected. The benefits will not be confined to English Literature. For instance, in English Language, in the section of your exam that asks you to read and respond to non-fiction texts, there will be a question on how writers use language. Students often do not realise that this tests similar skills to those learned in studying poetry, because it is asking you to show that you understand *how writers use words and literary techniques to influence the reader*.

Usually in the unseen question, you only have to write about one poem, but some examination boards ask you to compare two poems. Whichever form of question you have to answer, this book will provide you with carefully structured support that will build up your confidence and enable you to succeed.

How to use this book

This student book is divided into two sections:

- Section A: Reading poetry (Chapters 1–6)
- Section B: Making your skills count in the exam (Chapters 7–8).

Although each has a different focus, the chapters complement each other; what you learn in one will, almost certainly, have a bearing on what you learn in another, and sometimes you will be asked to think about links between features of poems studied in different chapters.

English is a skills-based subject, and skills are developed slowly (and reinforced) over long periods of time through practice in speaking and listening, and reading and writing. In working through the chapters that follow, you will be taking small but increasingly sure steps towards your final destination. This book does not provide you with 'answers', but with carefully structured activities that will enable you to develop key skills.

There is some challenging and stimulating literature in this book. It is inevitable that you will not like everything, but we are certain you will respond enthusiastically to the majority of texts, many of which you will be able to relate to your own experiences. In addition, your teachers have the freedom to choose poems for further study which they are enthusiastic about, and which they think you will find stimulating, to reinforce the skills taught in the book. They may even encourage you to nominate poems from collections you have read to study as a class or in a group. Enjoy!

A

Assessment Objectives

In this section you will have to:

respond to texts critically and imaginatively; select and evaluate relevant detail to illustrate and support interpretations (AO1)

explain how language, structure and form contribute to writers' presentation of ideas, themes and settings (AO2).

Exam tip

If you expect your teacher to provide you with 'right answers', you will not become an independent learner. The key to understanding a poem is *asking questions*: that is why group work plays such an important part in learning poetry appreciation skills – you can share your ideas with each other.

Reading poetry

Introduction

Students sometimes say that they don't like poetry, which is surprising. Think about song lyrics. These have a lot in common with poems. This poem by Elma Mitchell highlights the power that poetry can have:

> **This Poem…**
> This poem is dangerous: it should not be left
> Within the reach of children, or even of adults
> Who might swallow it whole, with possibly
> Undesirable side-effects. If you come across
> An unattended, unidentified poem
> In a public place, do not attempt to tackle it
> Yourself. Send it (preferably, in a sealed container)
> To the nearest centre of learning, where it will be rendered
> Harmless, by experts. Even the simplest poem
> May destroy your immunity to human emotions.
> All poems must carry a Government warning. Words
> Can seriously affect your heart.

How to read a poem

Poems need to be 'unpacked' in order to get to their meaning. This section of the book will help you to understand how to 'unpack' a poem. Although some poems can seem daunting at first, rereading them will lead to greater understanding and appreciation. Skills are learned by practice. Your teachers will provide you with good learning opportunities and you must take these. Being an active learner and taking pair and group work seriously will develop your self-confidence in interpreting poems. The more you read, the more experienced, capable and confident you will become.

In the exam

The unseen question in the exam will require you to write about a poem you have never read before. The unseen poetry essay that you will write in the exam will be assessed in relation to two Assessment Objectives – AO1 and AO2 – which are listed above.

This means that you will have to write about *what* the poet is saying – in terms of ideas as well as content – and *how* they say it, backing up your ideas by referring to the text.

If you are following an exam board that requires you to compare two poems, you will also be assessed on AO3, which you don't have to think about until your teacher prepares you specifically for the exam question. You will find support on writing comparative essays in Chapters 6 and 8.

This book will help you to meet the Assessment Objectives and achieve good marks. You will:

- examine particular methods poets use to express their experiences, ideas and feelings
- focus your reading on significant features of poems
- think about the effects on the reader of the language, structure and form used by poets.

Using this section

The techniques commonly used by poets are defined throughout the book. However, the focus is on interpreting the meaning of poems and explaining the effect of poets' techniques rather than listing **poetic devices**.

The best way to use this section is to study the chapters in order. In turn, it asks you to think about the following questions:

- **What** do poems 'mean' and why are they written?
- **Why** do poets choose particular words?
- **How** do poets create particular images?
- **How** do poets structure their poems?
- **Why** do poets choose particular verse forms?

The sixth chapter in this section explores how you can compare poems, which is an important skill in poetry analysis, even if you do not have to compare two unseen poems for your exam board.

You will be asked to annotate (make notes on) extracts from poems, and to write explanations of selected details. Practising these skills will be important as you prepare to write full-length essays in the exam.

By the time you reach the exam, you will have developed reading skills that you will apply automatically to poems, but here are some tips to help you to develop an approach to poetry.

- Read the title to see if it gives you any clues as to what the poem is about.
- Read the poem, without pausing over details, to gain some general understanding of its content.
- Reread the poem more slowly and in more detail, trying to understand it sentence by sentence, stanza by stanza.
- Ask yourself why the poet has chosen particular words and comparisons.
- Think about how the poem is organised into lines and stanzas.
- Think about the tone, mood and pace of the poem; reading it aloud may help.
- Think about the poet's intentions in writing the poem.

If you are not especially interested in poetry at the start of the course, hopefully you will be at the end!

Key terms

Poetic devices: these are the tools that the poets use in their writing; the techniques that help to communicate the ideas in the poem.

Exam tip

Remember that there are no 'right answers' when analysing poetry, only valid responses that must be backed up with evidence from the text.

1

Key terms

Interpret: work out the meaning or significance of a text.

Exam tip

Don't worry if you don't understand a poem on the first reading; asking questions and sharing ideas is an important part of interpreting poetry.

Getting to grips with poems

The purpose of this chapter is to develop your confidence in **interpreting** poems. It encourages you to ask and answer questions, and to back up your opinions, as you think about the meaning of a poem.

What does *meaning* mean? This may sound like a strange question, but there isn't necessarily a 'hard and fast' meaning to a poem. Different people might see a poem in slightly different ways, though they would probably agree on the 'core' of the poem's meaning. When you read a poem you try to interpret it. You can have different interpretations of a poem. It is important to note that there is no 'wrong' interpretation of a poem, as long as the interpretation can be backed up using evidence from the poem itself. You will practise this in more detail later in this chapter.

Your personal response to poetry is important, but you must be able to explain why you feel a certain way about a poem. Forming an interpretation of a poem can take time and you may need to reread poems several times, while asking questions about it, before you make up your mind. You may change your opinion of a poem the more you study it, so do not be afraid of exploring! As you work through this chapter and read more poetry, you will become more confident in discussing the meaning of poems and in supporting your views.

A. Thinking about questions

Read 'As Bad as a Mile' by Philip Larkin, and try to work out what you think it means. Consider:

- what it makes you think about
- how it makes you feel
- what the poet is trying to get you to think about.

As Bad as a Mile

Watching the shied core
Striking the basket, skidding across the floor,
Shows less and less of luck, and more and more

Of failure spreading back up the arm
Earlier and earlier, the unraised hand calm,
The apple unbitten in the palm.

Activities

1 Your first impression of a poem is the response you have after reading it for the first time. With a partner or in a small group, share your first impressions of what you think 'As Bad as a Mile' is about.

2 There may still be aspects of this poem that puzzle you. Think about and discuss the following questions (they may help you to 'unravel' the poem further).

- Why would anyone want to write about someone throwing an apple away?

- The speaker keeps just missing. If a footballer shoots and hits the post you'd say he was unlucky. What if he hit the post again and again? Is there any word in the poem you might be tempted to use instead of 'unlucky'?

- The word 'shied' in this poem may be unfamiliar to you. What is another word for 'shy', in the sense of a person throwing a ball at a coconut-shy? Find out what a coconut-shy is if you are unsure.

- The speaker thinks back to before he threw the apple. What might he be thinking and feeling?

3 Now see if you can write down a sentence that explains what Larkin is trying to say in the poem, and compare your answer with a partner's.

Stretch yourself

'As Bad as a Mile' was originally published with the title 'As Good as a Mile'. How do you think this change in title affects the meaning of the poem?

B. Asking your own questions

Learning to ask questions is the key to understanding poetry: you need to become a sort of 'poetry detective'. With practice, you'll build on the ability to ask questions that help you to develop your ideas.

In the last set of activities you were provided with questions to help you find clues to the meaning of a poem. You are now going to try to make up some questions of your own.

Read Mick Gowar's poem, 'Remembering St. Mary's Churchyard', on the next page several times, using the advice you were given in the Section introduction, page 3. Remember to think about:

- the title of the poem
- what the poem is about
- the words that the poet has chosen
- how the poem is organised
- the tone, mood and pace of the poem
- the intentions of the poet.

Remembering St. Mary's Churchyard

It took the two of us an hour or more to climb
the grass side of the hill
we stopped and started looped and
ran great circles in what adults thought
a ten minute walk at most

Between the fencing fringe of oaks
a sweep of grass for rolling in or flopping over dead
and up again at 'Ten' to fight
a path through Viking bracken
crisp as shredded wheat

Lords of the grassy slopes
all day all week all month we had
as far as we could see was ours
the sun would climb above the station
all day long through perfect blue

We climbed the churchyard gate and walked
into a garden in which time stood still
unrecognisable to us no lawns no concrete paths
no flowers we knew no stunted coloured clusters
but mysterious severe like stick-faced spinsters
dowdy speckled bell-shaped heads
and brittle feathered leaves
plants forgotten for a hundred years
We cut them down
and headed for the bench beneath the western wall
to eat our lunch

But never did
for she sat there
crying
with her hands unmoving in her lap
holding a pad of blank white paper
and a pencil

She never looked at us
She never moved
She never even
brought her hands up to her face
to hide her tears
She didn't care
what we might think of her
the mad girl crying on the bench
Not old not old like

Crazy Jack who screamed at cars
in St Anne's Road
but old enough to us
(Less than twenty)
in a summer frock
too tight
stretched taut across
a baby growing
big inside her

We knew that bulk
and what it meant
so what was there to cry about?
Why?
with her sketch pad
open untouched on her lap
Why should she cry
no shame no pride
not trying to stop
or even dry her tears

It didn't seem important
but we walked away as quietly as we could
and in the afternoon
forgot her

Activities

1 Write down five questions that you think would help someone else to understand the main ideas in 'Remembering St. Mary's Churchyard'; for example, 'Who is speaking in the poem?' Exchange your questions with a partner. In turn, answer each other's questions, backing up your answers by referring to the text.

2 Now see if you can agree on the poet's **intentions** in writing the poem. Are there any particular ideas that he wants us to think about?

3 Write a couple of sentences that describe the speaker and his friend's behaviour and attitudes towards the girl, and how the poet shows their immaturity.

Key terms

Intention: what the poet is trying to make the reader think and feel.

Justify: provide evidence to back up and support your argument.

C. Backing up your ideas

Opinions are of little value unless they can be **justified**. If you tell the head teacher that 'School's rubbish!', there's not much they can do to help you. If you tell them it's rubbish because the heating doesn't work in your classroom – which makes it hard for you to concentrate – something can be done to improve the situation.

So far you have looked at asking questions about poems. In the next activity you are going to be looking at answers, or rather, your responses. In this activity you have to justify your interpretations.

Read 'A Woman's Work' by Dorothy Nimmo. The title gives you helpful clues about the poet's intentions in writing the poem.

A Woman's Work

Will you forgive me that I did not run
to welcome you as you came in the door?
Forgive I did not sew your buttons on
and left a mess strewn on the kitchen floor?
A woman's work is never done
and there is more.

The things I did I should have left undone
the things I lost that I could not restore;
Will you forgive I wasn't any fun?
Will you forgive I couldn't give you more?
A woman's work is never done,
and there is more.

I never finished what I had begun,
I could not keep the promises I swore,
so we fought battles neither of us won
and I said, "Sorry!" and you banged the door.
A woman's work is never done
and there is more.

But in the empty space now you are gone
I find the time I didn't have before.
I lock the house and walk out to the sun
where the sea beats upon a wider shore
and woman's work is never done,
not any more.

1 Copy out the table below. With a partner, discuss which of the statements about the poem you think are true, which you think are false, and which you are not sure about, then complete the table. You must justify your opinions by referring to the text. There are not necessarily 'right' answers to all questions. Even if you're not sure, be prepared to say why.

Statement	Response	Justification
The woman is sorry for how she has behaved. It's right that she should apologise.	False	Her husband expected her to do too much in the house and didn't seem to help her. Maybe she is being sarcastic?
She couldn't help her behaviour.		
She seems very insecure.		
She is weak.		
She is strong.		
She misses her husband.		
At the end, she goes to the seaside to make herself feel better.		
At the end, she is worse off than before.		
At the end, she is better off than before.		

Stretch yourself

Explain why the speaker in 'A Woman's Work' uses lots of questions in the early stages of the poem but lots of statements at the end. What does this show about her?

D. Developing an interpretation

By now you should have learned to be more confident in interpreting poems and justifying your thinking. Read 'The Locker' by John Lancaster and then answer the following questions.

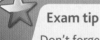

Exam tip

Don't forget to back up the points you make with evidence from the poem.

Activities

1 Work with a partner. Discuss briefly your first impressions of what you think the poem is about.

2 Who do you think is speaking in the poem? Read the poem more carefully, paying particular attention to the following details.

- 'she knew him by this ordinariness'
- 'The shock of the nude'
- 'Kept his ring on too'
- 'Tiredness … /Damping down the thrill of touch'
- 'She stands inside someone she thought she knew'
- 'Mother must never know'
- 'She wonders what they hide, like her'

3 Write a short account of the development of the woman's feelings in the poem that you could present to the class. Try to justify your ideas, for example:

At the start of the poem, the woman feels upset because the drive reminds her of the funeral procession as she is probably travelling slowly in a traffic jam, and is following a similar route. When she gets near to the works she thinks …

The Locker

The drive to the works was another cortege,
Numbing as the January sky
But without the undertaker droning on
About how the by-pass would speed things up.

Ordinariness clocked-up significance:
The bus-stop from where he'd rarely missed a shift,
The shop from where he'd bought them Friday sweets …
No great biography. But it all described his life,
Like going through his things:
The winter shirt he never wore;
The rack of chisels newly sharpened in the shed;
The row of pills which failed to do the trick;
The watch just got for thirty years.
Like the rest, she knew him by this ordinariness.

There could be nothing to expect
When the gate-man gave her the locker key.

The shock of the nude on the back of the door
Gave way to the usual list –
Overalls; some tools; a flask;
A plastic sandwich box; a pen;
A folded paper with horses underlined.
Then it fell from a book of Union rules.

Who was she? Pretty. Laughing.
And he looked happy holding hands.
Kept his ring on too.
On the back. A Blackpool photographer's stamp.
At a conference perhaps? A delegate friend?

But why'd he kept it all these years?
Perhaps things were not quite right at home,
The babies ill or waking in the night,
Time a blur of nappies, sick and crying,
Tiredness dulling the original ache,
Damping down the thrill of touch …
All too much. His one excursion. That would be it.
But he'd kept it hidden all these years.
Were there others?

For her, it was always what he stood for
More than what he said which counted.
Now all that gone,
She stands inside someone she thought she knew,
In her hand his secret self, the self
For which we lie like mad to keep concealed.

She tries again. Just a small deceit.
Mother must never know of course.
But a deceit it was. Though useless now.

But harm will not evaporate.
Each time she turns her eyes
Along the rows of lockers
She wonders what they hide, like her.

Check your learning

These poems have been chosen for you to study because they are thought-provoking. Choose the poem you have found the most interesting from this chapter and:

- explain why you enjoyed it

- explain what it made you think about and how it made you feel

- think of a question you would like to ask the author about the poem (for example, something to do with how it came to be written)

- explain in a paragraph what you think the meaning of the poem is, using evidence from the poem to support your interpretation.

Exam tip

Think about your personal response to each of the poems you read; it is important that you demonstrate this thinking when you come to your exam.

2

Word choices

Key terms

Tone: feelings, mood or atmosphere suggested by words.

In this chapter you will be looking at poets' choices of particular words, often as part of a pattern to create mood and atmosphere.

A. Communicating feelings

You can frequently tell a person's mood by his or her **tone** of voice and choice of language. When we use language, our choice of words can communicate feelings as well as information, and poets often deliberately select words to create atmosphere and/or suggest people's feelings about a situation.

For instance, if a writer were describing Christmas dinner and said, 'The *sweet aroma* of turkey and ham arose from the *gleaming silver* dishes', the choice of descriptive language would make the reader feel a positive sense of anticipation about the meal. If, on the other hand, the writer chose different words, such as, 'The *sickly smell* of *greasy* turkey and ham rose up from the *chipped* and *grubby-looking* plates', the reader might feel that the meal was unappealing.

Activity

1   a   Rewrite the following sentence, changing words and phrases to create positive feelings in the reader about a teenager getting up in the morning. Focus on the words underlined: 'The <u>bleary-eyed</u> girl <u>dragged</u> herself out of her <u>crumpled</u> bed, startled into life by the <u>clashing</u> of milk bottles.'

    b   Rewrite the following sentence, changing words and phrases to create negative feelings in the reader about a night-time scene. Focus on the words underlined: 'The <u>shining</u> moon appeared in the <u>beautiful</u> night sky above the <u>serene</u> landscape, casting <u>interesting</u> shadows on the ground.'

B. Creating mood

Read 'Conquerors' by Henry Treece. Essentially, the poem describes a village that a group of soldiers passes through on the way home from battle. In Activity A1, you will have noticed that many of the words that created mood and atmosphere were **adjectives**. The adjectives chosen by the poet in 'Conquerors' (for example, 'tired', 'sorry', 'blackened', 'melancholy') create the impression that the soldiers are weary and depressed by the weather and their surroundings.

Key terms

Adjective: a word that describes people or objects.

Conquerors

By sundown we came to a hidden village
Where all the air was still
And no sound met our tired ears, save
For the sorry drip of rain from blackened trees
And the melancholy song of swinging gates.
Then through a broken pane some of us saw
A dead bird in a rusting cage, still
Pressing his thin tattered breast against the bars,
His beak wide open. And
As we hurried through the weed-grown street,
A gaunt dog started up from some dark place
And shambled off on legs as thin as sticks
Into the wood, to die at least in peace.
No one had told us victory was like this;
Not one amongst us would have eaten bread
Before he'd filled the mouth of the grey child
That sprawled, stiff as stone, before the shattered door.
There was not one who did not think of home.

Activity

1   Pick out another five adjectives that create a similarly unattractive impression of the scene and the soldiers' mood, and discuss with a partner how they make the reader feel.

Now look closely at the extended description of the dead bird. You might **annotate** this section of the poem as follows.

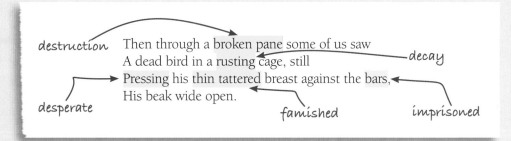

If you were writing about the effects the poet intended to create in this section, you might say something like:

The poet is trying to create a picture of desolation and decay by using phrases such as 'broken pane' and 'rusting cage'. He makes us feel sorry for the untidy, starved bird ('thin tattered breast'), which seems desperate to escape from captivity.

Perhaps the bird reflects the village's situation, starved and confined, and it is worth noting that only 'some of us saw'; most of the soldiers are too weary to notice all the details of their surroundings.

Activities

2 Now focus on the extended description of the dog ('And / As we hurried … in peace'). Write the poem down and annotate this section. Then write a comment explaining what effects the poet is trying to achieve, as in the example above. Use short quotations to back up your points.

Compare what you have written with a partner's comment. Has either one of you mentioned something not covered by the other? If so, add this to your notes.

3 Presumably the war is over and the child at the end is an enemy casualty. Read this section again and consider how people can behave differently in war and peacetime. What do you think the description of the speaker's feelings towards the child is intended to make the reader think about the experience of war? Write your answer to this question, giving clear reasons for your response.

4 Reread the last five lines of the poem. Now think about the poem's title. Decide which of the following you think best sums up why the poet chose the title, and explain your choice to a partner:

- because the soldiers are celebrating a victory
- to show that nobody actually 'wins' a war
- to show that their experiences have changed the soldiers' attitudes to war.

C. Thinking about titles

The title of a poem often gives the reader clues about what a poem is likely to be about. In the case of 'Conquerors', the title proves slightly misleading. Here, the poet uses **irony**; he uses a positive-sounding title to introduce the opposite, a description of a negative experience.

Key terms

Irony: the humorous or mildly sarcastic use of words to imply the opposite of what is being said.

Activities

1 What does the title 'Conquerors' suggest to you? How does this contrast with the content of the poem?

2 The title of the next poem, 'Night Nurses in the Morning', by Sheenagh Pugh, offers more straightforward clues about the poem's subject matter.

a What do you think the poem might be about?

b Imagine that, on the bus to school, you see a group of nurses get on the bus after finishing their night shift. Jot down a few words and phrases that might describe their appearance, mood and behaviour and compare ideas with a partner. What feelings did your notes convey?

Now read 'Night Nurses in the Morning'.

Night Nurses in the Morning

No bench in the bus shelter; they slump
against caving perspex, dragging the Silk Cut

deep into their lungs, eyes closed, holding
the moment, then letting a long breath go.

And they don't talk. Swollen ankles above
Big white boat-shoes, dreams of foot-spas.

Pale pink pale green pale blue, even without
the washed-out uniforms you could tell them

from us other early-morning faces
going in, starting the day. We eye them sideways

as they fall into seats, ease their shoes off.
More pallid than colliers or snooker players,

the vampires of mercy. All their haunts lie near
this bus route: here's St Stephen's Hospice,

where folk go to die, there, the Lennox Home
for Elderly Ladies. Just round the bend,

the other granny-park, where I walked past
an open window one evening when the lilac

was out, and heard a young voice scream, over and over,
You bitch, you bitch, and another tone,

querulous and high, a complaining descant
to her theme. They both sounded desperate.

People who live by night aren't quite canny.
We let them keep things running, avoid their eyes,

resenting the way they don't seem to need us there.
What do you do, in the corners of darkness

where we sweep the inconvenient? What is it
you never say to each other on the bus?

As our faces wake, exhaustion silvers
the backs of their eyes: not windows but mirrors.

Exam tip

As well as simply interpreting
individual words, think about
the effects of a sequence or
pattern of words in building up
a mood or atmosphere.

D. Descriptive language

The opening of the poem is quite abrupt ('No bench'), and the opening visual description is vivid ('they slump against caving perspex'). The nurses can hardly stand up ('slump'), and the wall of the shelter hardly supports their leaning weight ('caving perspex'). The rest of the opening sentence is very effective in showing their feelings. Annotation of the rest of the opening might go something like this:

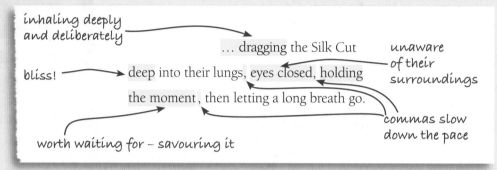

In an essay, you might comment on the poet's use of language as follows:

> The poet emphasises the intense pleasure and relief experienced by the nurses as they smoke their first cigarettes. Their eyes are closed, as if they've entered another heavenly world. They want to extract every morsel of enjoyment ('holding/the moment'), and the poet deliberately uses lots of commas, which slow down the pace of the lines to reflect how the nurses try to make the cigarettes last.

Activity

1 The first seven **stanzas** of this poem mainly focus on describing the appearance and mood of the nurses. Look at the examples below and discuss with a partner what makes these descriptive details effective.

- '... Swollen ankles above
  Big white boat-shoes, dreams of foot-spas.'
- 'Pale pink pale green pale blue, even without
  the washed-out uniforms ...'
- 'More pallid than colliers or snooker players,
  the vampires of mercy.'

Choose the description you consider the most effective and annotate it as above. Then write a comment on what effects the poet creates by her choice of language.

It is worth pausing after 'vampires of mercy' and reflecting on the impression of the nurses created by the poet. The picture is of a group of people doing a demanding and important job whose value is not always recognised by the public. They are nocturnal creatures who are slightly mysterious; they seem self-contained, but strong and independent.

In the second half of the poem the poet concentrates on people's attitudes towards the nurses' work.

Activities

2 Discuss with a partner the attitudes that are suggested by the following details:

- 'granny-park'
- 'They both sounded desperate.'
- *'in the corners of darkness / where we sweep the inconvenient'*.

Do these details suggest that the speaker is sympathetic towards the patients, or not?

3 The last two lines 'summarise' the key ideas explored in the poem. Using the following questions to help you, write an explanation of what the poet is saying about the nurses and the public's relationship with them. (Before writing, think about the ideas that have been developed so far in the poem.)

- What is the connection between 'wake' and 'exhaustion'?
- What is the difference between 'windows' and 'mirrors'?
- How might the poet be using 'silver' in two senses?

This poem has a form of organisation typical of many poems. It:

- begins with description ('setting the scene')
- develops thoughts/ideas about the situation
- concludes with a key thought or idea that the poet wants us to reflect on.

Stretch yourself

Write a short explanation of how the author of one of the two poems in this chapter made you feel sympathy for the people in the poems.

E. The sounds of words

Words are very subtle; they have sound qualities as well as meaning, and poets often use the sounds suggested by particular words – or sequences of words – to create particular effects in their writing.

Some words echo their meaning in their sound; they sound like the idea being expressed, for example 'splash' and 'crunch'. The use of such words by a poet is called **onomatopoeia**.

Sometimes a poet will repeat the same **consonant** at the beginnings of several words that are close together. This technique is called **alliteration**. Sometimes this just helps to add emphasis to a phrase, for example 'stiff as a stone' in 'Conquerors'. Sometimes it can be used for more subtle effect, as when Wilfred Owen uses the phrase 'rifles' rapid rattle' to suggest the sound and speed of machine-gun fire.

Similarly (but less obviously) a poet sometimes repeats a vowel sound in words close together for emphasis. For example, in describing a rat's '*t*apered t*ai*l', Seamus Heaney uses **assonance** as well as the more obvious alliteration to emphasise the descriptive detail.

It is less important that you know the terms than that you can explain how poets use sound effects in language in your own words.

Activity

1 The following are examples of these three sound techniques, accompanied by brief explanations of how they fit into the context of the poem they are taken from. Discuss with a partner the sound effects the poets are trying to create by using the chosen words.

- Onomatopoeia: 'Bubbles gargled delicately'. (The poet is writing about a pond inhabited by tadpoles.)
- Alliteration: 'In the greyness / and drizzle of one despondent / dawn'. (The poet is describing a dull morning.)
- Assonance: 'a mate / with a mind as cold as the slice of ice / within my own brain'. (The poet is describing a 'tough' teenager's thoughts about building a snowman.)

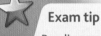

Exam tip

Reading poems aloud will help you to hear the effect of the sounds that the poet has chosen.

F. Sounds and sound patterns

At the opening of his poem 'South Cumberland, 10th May 1943', Norman Nicholson describes an unusually late snowfall as follows:

> The fat flakes fall
> In parachute invasion from the yellow sky.

If you were writing about the poet's use of language here you might say something like:

> As well as using colour to describe the lurid sky and suggesting how the white flakes meander down to take over the land (in the phrase 'parachute invasion'), the poet also suggests the soft delicacy of the snow by repeating soft consonant sounds in the phrase 'fat flakes fall'.

The opening of Ted Hughes's poem 'Thistles' goes as follows:

> Every one a revengeful burst
> Of resurrection, a grasped fistful
> Of splintered weapons and Icelandic frost thrust up
>
> From the underground stain of a decayed Viking.

If you were writing about the poet's use of language in this extract, you might say something like:

> As well as suggesting the spikiness of the thistles by comparing them to sharp weapons, the pattern of consonants used by the poet ('sp', 'f', 'st', 'c' and 't') give the description a 'spiky' sound in the highlighted extract.

Studying the two extracts above shows how consonants can sound different in different contexts, the 'f' sound being soft in the first example and harsh in the second.

Activities

1 The following extracts are further examples of poets using the sounds of words, usually in patterns, to add to intended meaning. With a partner, discuss what sort of sound effects you think the poets are trying to create. (Reading them aloud a few times will help.)

a

Yet still the unresting castles thresh
In fullgrown thickness every May.
Last year is dead, they seem to say,
Begin afresh, afresh, afresh.

(The poet is describing trees coming into leaf.)

b

... the flung spray hits
The very windows, spits like a tame cat
Turned savage.

(The poet is describing a ferocious storm.)

c

Sudden successive bullets streak the silence

(The poet is describing soldiers waiting in the trenches for the enemy's next move.)

d

... the warm thick slobber
Of frogspawn

(The poet is describing a young boy collecting frogspawn.)

e

... Some hopped:
The slap and plop were obscene threats.

(The poet is describing the same boy's fear when he sees fully grown frogs for the first time.)

2 Choose one of these examples and write a short explanation of how the poet uses sounds in the extract, modelling your answer on the examples of comments you read earlier.

Check your learning

In this chapter you have learned that words do not only describe or give information, they can also be used to *affect the reader's attitudes and feelings* about people and situations. When a series of words and phrases is used to build up a 'bigger picture', a poet can create a particular *mood* or *atmosphere*, which can be positive or negative. The sounds of the words chosen by the poet also have an impact on the reader.

In the following short extract, from John Mole's poem 'The Classroom', what impression of the atmosphere in the classroom is the poet trying to create? Write a short explanation, referring to words and phrases from the extract to support your interpretation.

Desk-lids deafen the dead with chaotic clatter,
Crisp-packets crackle and crinkle, a galaxy of gobstoppers
Glop and gurgle in cheeks blown big as bellies.

Creating pictures with words

Key terms

Image: a picture created with a poet's choice of words that the reader can imagine.

Visualise: to picture or to see in the imagination.

In this chapter you are going to practise interpreting poets' use of images and develop your understanding of how they are used.

A. Poetic images

Just as an artist can create a picture using brush and paint, a poet can use words to create a picture in the reader's imagination. We are aware of the world around us through our five senses, especially our sense of sight. Poets often use language to appeal to our sense of sight and create pictures that we can **visualise**.

For example, what would you think of if you were asked to describe a railway line? Study the annotated image below, taken from Seamus Heaney's poem 'Dawn Shoot'.

Poet looking down railway line towards bridge; shape suggests a staring eye.

'Scored' also suggests railway line really stands out, like a line drawn forcefully with a pen.

The rails scored a bull's eye into the eye

Of a bridge.

Line is dead straight, direct; hits its 'target' like an arrow.

Repetition of 'eye' to reinforce image.

Activity

1 Now that you have studied this poetic image, write a full explanation of what the poet is trying to get the reader to imagine, referring to words and phrases. For example, *This image suggests to me …*

In 'Journey from Hull', Grace Nichols describes a train from a different viewpoint:

our inter-city boa pushing

through the deepening night

Activity

2 Write out the quotation and annotate it as in the Heaney example. Pay particular attention to the highlighted words. Compare your notes with a partner's, then write a sentence explaining what this image suggests to you. (Make sure you know what a boa constrictor is first!)

B. Snapshots of scenes

'Calendar' by Owen Sheers is short and simply organised. It provides the reader with 'snapshots' of the seasons, creating very visual images or 'word-pictures' of aspects of scenes typical of the four seasons. Read 'Calendar' closely.

Calendar

Spring
Swallows crotchet and
minim the telephone wires,
sing volts down the line.

Summer
Bees go down at the
lips of foxgloves, nervous like
a lover's first time.

Autumn
A spider has danced
a fingerprint in the space
between two branches.

Winter
Nests clot in the veins
of the tree – the rooks are a
passing infection.

Activities

1 The poem has 12 lines, the description of each season having three lines with subheadings. Why do you think the poet chose to organise the poem in this way?

2 Read 'Calendar' again and think about the 'pictures' created in each stanza. Study the sample comments below on the scene described in the first stanza:

Spring: The poet sees the telephone wires as being like lines on sheet music, with the swallows perched on the lines like crotchets and minims (musical symbols) because of their rounded bodies and pointing tails. He imagines their songs being transmitted down the wires like charges of electricity ('volts').

With a partner, discuss your impressions of the scenes described in the last three stanzas. Choose the one you find most interesting/effective, and write your own explanation of how the language used helps you to imagine the scene.

Stretch yourself

Now create your own image. Write three lines in which you aim to capture some aspect of one of the seasons, for example describing the effects of weather. It need not be in Britain – it could be entitled something like 'Christmas in Cairo'.

C. Language choices

When reading 'Calendar', you might have felt that the atmosphere created in 'Winter' was slightly sinister. The poet created a visual picture of the season, but the word 'infection' made the rooks seem rather unpleasant and almost threatening. This word is **emotive**.

Study the photograph of a child in a developing country and think about how it is intended to make you feel.

As you are now aware, poets can create pictures with words, and they can affect your feelings. In 'The Face of Hunger', the poet, Oswald Mbuyiseni Mtshali, uses words to create a picture similar to that in the photograph; he is also trying to affect our feelings.

The poem has been printed below with some key words and phrases omitted.

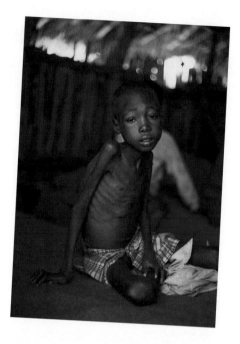

The Face of Hunger

I counted the ribs on his concertina chest
bones protruding as if chiselled
by a sculptor's hand of famine.

He looked with glazed pupils
seeing only a bun on some _____1_____ shelf.

The skin was pale and taut
like _____2_____

His tongue darted in and out
like _____3_____
snatching a _____4_____ of flies.

O! child,
your stomach is _____5_____
roaring day and night.

Words omitted:

a) confetti

b) sky-high

c) a glove on a doctor's hand

d) a den of lions

e) a chameleon's

Activities

1 With a partner, discuss which of the words and phrases should go into which gaps in order for the poem to make sense (match numbers to letters). Think carefully about how the images help us to imagine the boy's appearance and situation. There is a complete copy of the poem on page 58 for you to compare your responses with.

2 Choose a word or phrase from the poem that you think is particularly powerful. Explain in writing what it helps you to imagine and how it makes you feel. For example:

> I think that 'seeing only a bun on some sky-high shelf' is very vivid and moving, because you can imagine the boy desperately longing for something he can never reach – and a bun is not very substantial food anyway.

Activity

3 Do you think that this poem is as effective as the photograph you looked at? Do you think that the photographer and the poet have the same intentions here? With a partner, discuss the emotive impact that the poem as a whole has on you.

D. Different types of image

You may have noticed that in 'The Face of Hunger' the poet uses images in slightly different ways. Sometimes he draws the reader's attention to the fact that he is making an imaginative comparison by using 'like' or 'as', for example when he compares the movement of the boy's tongue to that of a chameleon's, which 'darted in and out' because of his thirst. This is a **simile**.

At other times the poet describes one thing as another. An imaginative comparison is still being made, but it is *implied*. For example, when he uses the phrase 'concertina chest', he is suggesting that the boy is so undernourished that his ribs stick out like the folds of a concertina. This is a **metaphor**.

Any idea can be expressed as either a simile or metaphor and have a similar effect on the reader. A poet might say,

> 'The ship cut through the ocean <u>like</u> a plough cutting through soil'

(this is a simile), or equally – and more concisely –

> 'The ship <u>ploughed through</u> the ocean'

(this is a metaphor).

Both conjure up the same picture of a plough cutting a furrow and leaving churned-up water (like soil after a plough) in its wake (behind it).

What matters is not so much that you know these terms and can 'spot' similes and metaphors, but that you understand *why* the poet has chosen his words, and what *effect* the images have on the reader.

E. Extending an image

An image can make you *see* something in a different light; for example, in 'Calendar', how a spider's web could look like a fingerprint. An image can make you *feel* as well as see; for example, the reader feels sympathy for the boy in 'The Face of Hunger', whose rumbling stomach is a 'den of lions'. An image can also make you *think* – we often use 'see' to mean 'understand', as in 'Do you see what I mean?'

In 'The Thickness of Ice', the poet, Liz Loxley, uses skating as an image and *develops* it in detail, inviting the reader to think about how different aspects of skating are like different aspects of relationships. Read the poem over the page carefully, tracing the main idea through. Think particularly about the importance of the sections in brackets.

The Thickness of Ice

At first we will meet as friends
(Though secretly I'll be hoping
We'll become much more
And hoping that you're hoping that too).

At first we'll be like skaters
Testing the thickness of ice
(With each meeting
We'll skate nearer the centre of the lake).

Later we will become less anxious to impress,
Less eager than the skater going for gold,
(The triple jumps and spins
Will become an old routine:
We will be content with simple movements).

Later we will not notice the steady thaw,
The creeping cracks will be ignored,
(And one day when the ice gives way
We will scramble to save ourselves
And not each other).

Last of all we'll meet as acquaintances
(Though secretly we'll be enemies,
Hurt by missing out on a medal,
Jealous of new partners).

Last of all we'll be like children
Having learnt the thinness of ice,
(Though secretly, perhaps, we may be hoping
To break the ice between us
And maybe meet again as friends).

★ Exam tip

Think about how individual similes or metaphors in a poem contribute to the overall image created by the poet.

Activities

1. Look at the opening words of each stanza. What do they tell the reader about how the poem develops?

2. Brackets in writing are used to explain something more fully – often to make something more obvious. Here the sections in brackets represent secret thoughts that cannot always be admitted to the other person in the relationship. Copy out the table shown opposite and write notes on each stanza of the poem to show how the thoughts, feelings and behaviour of the couple change during the poem, both openly and secretly, and then compare notes with a partner.

Stanza	On the surface …	Deep down …
1	When we first meet we'll just behave like good friends.	But really, I'd like to get more serious; I hope you feel the same way.
2	To begin with, we'll be wary of each other and try to test how solid our relationship is (have we enough in common?).	But every time we meet, we'll take more risks and become more confident that we can 'make it' as a couple.
3		
4		
5		
6		

3 With a partner, discuss what evidence there is in the poem to back up the following statements.

The poet is saying that:

- beginning a new relationship is exciting, but you have to take risks to succeed
- people often don't behave naturally when they're attracted to a member of the opposite sex
- people don't always notice at the time the signs that their relationship is deteriorating
- love is such a strong emotion that it can turn to hate after separation.

4 Choose one of the statements and write an explanation of why you consider it to be true. For example, I think the poet is saying that beginning a new relationship is exciting, but you have to take risks to succeed because she says that the couple are 'testing' the ice and skate nearer to the dangerous centre of the lake 'with each meeting'. This suggests that the start of a new relationship is scary and could potentially hurt you, but it is also thrilling and exciting. If they had not tried to skate to the centre and overcome the risks, the couple may not have got together.

Exam tip

When interpreting images, don't just explain why an imaginative comparison has been made, explain its effects on the reader.

Check your learning

In this chapter you have learned that images can make you *see*, *feel* and *think* about a subject or situation more clearly. In addition, a poet sometimes develops an idea by inviting the reader to think about different aspects of a central image.

The following is an extract from an advertisement for a dating agency.

'Since Operation Match provides everything except the spark, it can't be held responsible if you burn your fingers.'

Think about the 'match' **pun**, and explain the meaning and effect of the image developed here by the writer.

Key terms

Pun: a play on words; deliberately using words that can have a double meaning. Often used for comical effect.

How poems are organised

Objectives

In this chapter you will:

learn how poets organise their ideas and descriptions

learn that poems often have a distinctive 'shape' that reinforces meaning.

Key terms

Structure: the shape and organisation of a poem.

In this chapter you are going to study how poets 'shape' poems; how they **structure** their writing to give their ideas and descriptions maximum impact.

A. A typical structure

When we refer to the structure of a building, we are talking about how it is *organised* – its floors, its rooms, its doors, its windows and so on. We are thinking of how it is put together and of how the parts relate to the whole.

When we talk about a poem's structure we mean:

- how the ideas and words are organised
- why they are organised in this way
- the effects of the organisation on the reader.

Read 'Street Gang' by H. Webster.

Poets often like to give the reader something to think about, much in the same way as teachers might tell a story with a moral in assembly. The structure of 'Street Gang' is typical of many poems. The poet:

- describes a situation ('sets the scene')
- goes on to describe a key event
- ends with a thought about what's happened.

Street Gang

Everywhere they are waiting. In silence.
In boredom. Staring into space.
Reflecting on nothing, or on violence
That is long since past. Wondering.
Wondering what will happen next.
Whatever it is is beyond their control
Or understanding. They are waiting. Not vexed
By any thoughts of the uncertain future
(Apparently); absorbed in the present
Shot through with spasms of the violent
Past. They are waiting. ...
                    Coffee-cups
Battle. Matches flare. Cigarettes
Glow in the darkness of the milk-bar
Or the drug-store. Hour after hour
They sit, indistinguishable
In the darkness: oblivious of who they are
Or what they want: except to be together.

Then suddenly it happens. A motor-cycle
Explodes outside, a cup smashes,
They are on their feet, identified
At last as living creatures.
The universal silence is shattered,
The law overthrown, chaos
Has come again ...
                    The victim has been kicked,
Gouged, stamped on, crucified.

His blood streams across the pavement.
And none of them knows why.
Tomorrow their endless vigil
Will begin again. Perhaps nothing will happen.
Or perhaps, this time, a single
Scapegoat will not suffice. ...

Activities

1 In the opening section of the poem, as well as describing the gang and where they 'hang out', the poet gives the reader hints about *why* the boys are just sitting around ('waiting' is repeated several times). 'In boredom' makes one aspect of their behaviour clear. There are two other important clues, the first of which is explained to you below. Write an explanation of the second, and compare your ideas with a partner's.

a

> '…Not vexed
> By any thoughts of the uncertain future
> (Apparently); absorbed in the present …'

Comment:

The members of the gang don't seem to have any purpose in life; they just live for the moment and don't think about the consequences of their behaviour. Perhaps they're unemployed, or low-achievers who don't think they have a future.

b

> 'They sit, indistinguishable
> In the darkness: oblivious of who they are
> Or what they want: except to be together.'

Comment:

The gang members …

2 After 'Then suddenly …' the poet describes the key event: the vicious attack. Endings are also important. In the last five lines the poet reflects on what has happened – but without pointing out a definite moral or message. Discuss with a partner whether you agree with the following possible interpretations, and say why.

The poet is suggesting that:

- the gang's violence is senseless
- we need to tackle the causes of the gang's behaviour
- the violence was probably just an isolated incident
- there's no hope for these boys.

Choose one statement that you agree with and write down your explanation, referring closely to the poem (*The reason I think that (choose statement) is true is that …*). Compare your answer with a partner's.

3 Note how the **pace** of 'Street Gang' changes. In the opening long description there are lots of short, incomplete sentences without verbs, and lots of pauses that slow down the pace of the poem. How does the pace change with the description of the attack? How has the poet achieved this?

Exam tip

The endings of poems are often significant; poets will sometimes give hints here about their intentions in writing the poem.

Key terms

Pace: the speed at which a poem 'flows'.

B. Using contrast

Contrast is a simple but very effective method of making things stand out. Instead of painting all the walls of a room the same colour, people often paint different walls in different colours so that each colour draws attention to itself; or they choose furniture and wallpaper to create contrasts of dark and light. Poets often use similar methods to achieve similar effects.

Read 'The Boys and Girls Are Going out to Play' by Dorothy Nimmo. The poet explores the contrast between the behaviour of boys and girls by carefully arranging the stanzas.

Key terms

Contrast: poets use contrast when inviting readers to compare two things.

The Boys and Girls Are Going out to Play

The boys and girls are going out to play.

The boys make guns with sticks and blaze away,
imaginary birds flop from the sky.

The girls make houses out of bales of hay,
their skipping games are based on courtship rhymes.

The boys are battering brambles on their way
and slashing trees that hang across the ride.

The girls are ponies all the summer's day
constructing jumps from stakes and garden twine.

The boys are doing wheelies on their bikes
they twist each other's arms behind their backs.

The girls read True Life stories, pick their spots,
iron their blouses, fight their mums and cry.

The boys have big bikes now. Their helmets hide
their private faces. They bomb up the lane.

The girls go soft with love all dressed in white
their mothers think this is their proudest day.

The boys meet brick walls head on. And they might
Pull through. Or not. They go the bravest way.

The girls meet life head on and they survive
to watch the children going out to play.

Whichever way they go they go away.

Exam tip

Remember to look at how stanzas are arranged and how they develop ideas and descriptions.

26

You are used to structuring your own writing; you organise your writing into paragraphs with 'topics'. In poetry, a stanza serves a similar function to that of a paragraph: it enables the reader to pause, take in, and reflect on a section of writing before moving on. Stanzas are the most obvious organisational feature of poems.

Activities

1 This is a poem that has a distinctive 'shape' because of its short stanzas. With a partner, discuss the following questions.

   a The single opening line introduces the situation (repeating the title), and then the boys' and girls' behaviour at different stages of their lives is described as they grow up. How does the girls' behaviour compare with the boys'?

   b The poet describes the boys' and girls' behaviour in alternating stanzas. What effect does this have on the reader?

2 You have learned that poems often lead up to a final important thought or idea. Like the first line, the final single line describes the boys' and girls' behaviour. Who do you think might be speaking, and what might he/she be thinking and feeling?

3 Complete the following statements about the poem's structure, using the first example as a model.

   ● The short opening line is a simple statement intended to 'set the scene'.

   ● The purpose of the main section, with its two-line stanzas, is to …

   ● The purpose of the last line, which is single and stands out, is to …

Stretch yourself

How does this poem make you feel about gender stereotypes of girls and boys? Does the use of contrast affect this?

C. Out of order

The most common way for a piece of writing to be structured is **chronologically**. In 'The Boys and Girls Are Going out to Play', for instance, the poem follows the children's lives as they grow up.

The next poem, by Wilfred Owen, is set during the First World War. For love of their country, young men – often under the legal enlistment age of 16 – flocked to Europe to fight the Germans. They were innocent about the horrors of war. Tragically, most of them did not come back.

Key terms

Chronological: in time sequence; the order in which things happen.

As explained earlier, a stanza is like a paragraph. The poem 'Disabled' by Wilfred Owen is printed below, but the stanzas have been jumbled up.

a With a partner, rearrange the stanzas into the order in which you think the poet wrote them. Thinking about the ends and beginnings of stanzas will help you.

b Compare the order that you and your partner have selected with another pair and explain your choices.

Disabled

A One time he liked a blood-smear down his leg,
After the matches, carried shoulder-high.
It was after football, when he'd drunk a peg,
He thought he'd better join. – He wonders why.
Someone had said he'd look a god in kilts,
That's why; and may be, too, to please his Meg;
Aye, that was it, to please the giddy jilts
He asked to join. He didn't have to beg;
Smiling they wrote his lie; aged nineteen years.
Germans he scarcely thought of; all their guilt,
And Austria's, did not move him. And no fears
Of Fear came yet. He thought of jewelled hilts
For daggers in plaid socks; of smart salutes;
And care of arms; and leave; and pay arrears;
Esprit de corps; and hints for young recruits.
And soon, he was drafted out with drums and cheers.

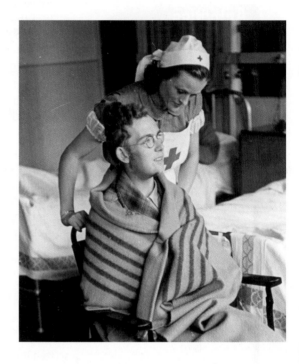

B About this time Town used to swing so gay
When glow-lamps budded in the light blue trees,
And girls glanced lovelier as the air grew dim, –
In the old times, before he threw away his knees.
Now he will never feel again how slim
Girls' waists are, or how warm their subtle hands;
All of them touch him like some queer disease.

D He sat in a wheeled chair, waiting for dark,
And shivered in his ghastly suit of grey,
Legless, sewn short at elbow. Through the park
Voices of boys rang saddening like a hymn,
Voices of play and pleasure after day,
Till gathering sleep had mothered them from him.

C Now, he will spend a few sick years in Institutes,
And do what things the rules consider wise,
And take whatever pity they may dole.
To-night he noticed how the women's eyes
Passed from him to the strong men that were whole.
How cold and late it is! Why don't they come
And put him into bed? Why don't they come?

E There was an artist silly for his face,
For it was younger than his youth, last year.
Now, he is old; his back will never brace;
He's lost his colour very far from here,
Poured it down shell-holes till the veins ran dry,
And half his lifetime lapsed in the hot race,
And leap of purple spurted from his thigh.

F Some cheered him home, but not as crowds cheer Goal.
Only a solemn man who brought him fruits
Thanked him; and then inquired about his soul.

Activities

2 Now study the poem in the original sequence from the copy on page 56. Compare the sequences of stanzas you chose in Activity C1 with the original version. How close were you? Now write brief notes on what each stanza is about and compare your responses with a partner.

3 Discuss which parts of the poem describe the present, and which the past. The poet reveals details of the boy's past gradually. How does the reader feel about the boy's tragedy on learning the following details?

- He was so handsome that artists wanted to paint him.
- He was a good sportsman.
- He thought that being a soldier would impress the girls.
- He lied about his age, and the recruiting officer 'turned a blind eye'.

4 You will have noticed that in stanzas 2–4 the poet contrasts the past when the boy was innocent, with the present, now that he is disabled. From each of those three stanzas, find and write down one detail that is a positive description of the past, and one that is a negative description of the present. Compare your selected quotations with a partner's.

5 In this poem the poet doesn't 'tell the story' from beginning to end, but deliberately opens with a dramatic description of the boy's disability that he suffered later in life. Owen does this to shock the reader and convey the horrors of war from the outset. How does the poet make the opening stanza shocking?

6 You have learned that poems often lead up to a final key thought or idea. This poem is unusual in that it ends in a series of exclamations and questions. How does this make the reader feel about the boy's situation?

> **Exam tip**
>
> Look at the number of lines in the stanzas of a poem. If any stanzas are considerably shorter or longer than others in the poem, look at these carefully. The poet may be wishing to draw the reader's attention to these lines in particular.

Check your learning

In this chapter you have learned how poets emphasise meaning by the way they organise their ideas. The following is a short descriptive poem by R. S. Thomas.

Write a paragraph explaining how the poet organises his ideas to make his description more vivid.

Night and Morning

One night of tempest I arose and went
Along the Menai shore on dreaming bent;
The wind was strong, and savage swung the tide,
And the waves blustered on Caernarfon side.

But on the morrow, when I passed that way,
On Menai shore the hush of heaven lay;
The wind was gentle and the sea a flower,
And the sun slumbered on Caernarfon tower.

5

Key terms

Form: a poem's printed 'shape'. For example, the sonnet form is a poem of 14 lines. Poets select the poetic form that best enhances the meaning of their poem.

The best words in the best order

In this chapter you will learn how poets organise ideas and descriptions into particular lines and verse **forms** to reinforce meaning.

A. Poems that rhyme

When poets write in rhyme, it is almost inevitable that the reader will focus on the words that rhyme at the ends of lines. Read 'Another Christmas Poem' by Wendy Cope.

Letters of the alphabet are generally used to identify the rhyme pattern in a poem. Each new final sound is given a new letter. Here the first and third lines rhyme, as do the second and fourth, so they are indicated by the same letter. A fresh sound at the end of line 5, if there were one, would become 'c', and so on.

The rhyme in the second and fourth lines of 'Another Christmas Poem' helps to emphasise key phrases, which are contrasted: the 'loving cup' sounds positive; 'washing-up' does not, and ends the poem in a neatly humorous way.

Now read 'Wires' by Philip Larkin.

Another Christmas Poem

Bloody Christmas, here again.	a
Let us raise a loving cup:	b
Peace on earth, goodwill to men,	a
And make them do the washing-up.	b

Wires

The widest prairies have electric fences,	a
For though old cattle know they must not stray	b
Young steers are always scenting purer water	c
Not here, but anywhere. Beyond the wires	d
Leads them to blunder up against the wires	d
Whose muscle-shredding violence gives no quarter.	c
Young steers become old cattle from that day,	b
Electric limits to their widest senses.	a

 Activities

 1 With a partner, discuss:

- why the young cattle like to wander
- what happens to them
- how this affects their behaviour
- why old cattle behave differently.

2 Could the cattle represent people? If the poem is about the behaviour of young and old people, what might the fences and electric shocks represent? Discuss with a partner.

Activities

3 Study the **rhyme-scheme** of the poem. Discuss whether you agree with the following statements.

The poet wrote the poem in this way because:

- the rhyme suggests the mechanical plodding of the cattle
- the rhyme-scheme reflects the idea of lack of progress in the poem: the rhyme 'goes back on itself' just as the cattle move outwards and back
- it helps him to emphasise the contrasts of freedom and restriction in the opening and closing lines.

4 With a partner, discuss the following statements and whether you think they are relevant to the poem.

- If we didn't have rules and laws, there'd be chaos in society.
- You need to take some risks to understand danger.
- You need freedom to discover your potential.

Stretch yourself

In the first and last lines of 'Wires', the phrases 'The widest prairies' and 'Electric limits' are placed prominently. Write an explanation of what the poet is trying to emphasise about the situation of the cattle (and people) in using these phrases in this way.

B. Word placement

Although rhyme often has the effect of emphasising the final words or phrases in lines, the openings of lines are very important too. When poets want to emphasise key ideas, they often place the important words at the beginnings or ends of lines because the reader's eye is naturally drawn to openings and endings.

Word placement and rhyme-scheme help to give a poem its **rhythm**, which can add to the poem's meaning. A slower rhythm can make the ideas presented in a poem seem more gentle, whereas a fast rhythm can make a poem's ideas more dramatic and exciting.

'Drummer Hodge' by Thomas Hardy, on the next page, is about the death of a young soldier abroad in Africa during the Boer War. His death is particularly tragic because a drummer would be unarmed and unable to defend himself. Wessex is an old name for Dorset, and the Karoo is a desert in South Africa.

Exam tip

It is important to examine all parts of a poem carefully, but it can be useful to look at the openings and endings of lines – that's often where you'll find the key ideas of a poem.

Drummer Hodge

They throw in Drummer Hodge, to rest
Uncoffined – just as found:
His landmark is a kopje-crest
That breaks the veldt around;
And foreign constellations west
Each night above his mound.

Young Hodge the Drummer never knew –
Fresh from his Wessex home –
The meaning of the broad Karoo,
The Bush, the dusty loam,
And why uprose to nightly view
Strange stars amid the gloam.

Yet portion of that unknown plain
Will Hodge for ever be;
His homely Northern breast and brain
Grow to some Southern tree,
And strange-eyed constellations reign
His stars eternally.

Activities

1. Remembering what you have learned, work out the rhyming pattern of the poem and give each line an appropriate letter.

2. The three stanzas have three distinct rhyming patterns and describe three distinct 'topics'. Write down a phrase that sums up what each stanza is about and share your ideas with a partner.

3. With a partner, discuss what the poet wants the reader to think and feel about Hodge from his use of 'They throw' and 'Uncoffined' at the beginning of the first stanza. How does the positioning of these words make them forceful?

4. In the first two stanzas, the poem is rather negative in tone – creating sympathy for his unceremonial burial, his innocence, and his separation from home. What does the word 'Yet' at the opening of stanza 3 prepare the reader for?

5. Each stanza ends with a reference to the stars. What is the poet suggesting about Hodge's situation in each of them?

6. A comment on the poet's technique at the opening of the poem might read:

   The placing of 'They throw' at the very start of the first line of the poem emphasises that Hodge was worthless; he was shown no respect as a human being.

   Choose a word or phrase placed at either the beginning or end of one of the last three lines of the poem and write a similar comment on how that word or phrase helps to end the poem on a positive note.

C. Free verse

Free verse is poetry that has no regular pattern of rhyme. It is called free verse because it enables poets to arrange their thoughts into lines without restriction (often emphasising key words or images at the openings or ends of lines) and to use lengths of lines to create effects, for example a single-word line to emphasise a key word or phrase.

Read 'The Pond' by Owen Sheers.

The Pond

This place where I took things,
sunk shallow in the middle of the field,
a secret bruise hidden by trees.

Where I brought my grandfather's death,
sucking squash from a shrinking carton,
while the tears dried to slug lines over my cheeks.

And my first kiss, in the arched iron cow-shed,
gum-stitched and tense,
as the light faded and the farms lit up.

Where I carried my arguments,
vowing never to return, hunching under the oak,
only to slink back

through the long grass, brushing up to my knees,
when the cold had dug deep in my bones
and my anger had evolved into hunger.

Activities

1 The first two stanzas have been annotated below with some questions to help you think about the meaning and effect of selected details. Write brief notes in response to the questions and share your ideas with a partner.

What do these three details suggest and how are they given emphasis?

This place where I took things,
sunk shallow in the middle of the field,
a secret bruise hidden by trees.

Where I brought my grandfather's death,
sucking squash from a shrinking carton,
while the tears dried to slug lines over my cheeks.

What sort of things?

What does this image help you to imagine?

2 Study the annotation of stanza 3 printed below – you are given comments this time.

So nervous he couldn't relax; short line gives image emphasis.

And my first kiss, in the arched iron cow-shed,
gum-stitched and tense,
as the light faded and the farms lit up.

Balanced line creates neat contrast.

The last two stanzas have not been annotated, but details have been highlighted for you to think about. Make your own notes on the effects of the poet's positioning of words, then exchange ideas with a partner.

Where I carried my arguments,
vowing never to return, hunching under the oak,
only to slink back

through the long grass, brushing up to my knees,
when the cold had dug deep in my bones
and my anger had evolved into hunger.

only to slink back

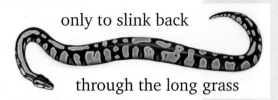

through the long grass

You may have noticed that in a free verse poem the poet often doesn't end a sentence at the end of a line, but extends it on to the next line. Sentences can begin on one line and 'snake' around to the next line either within the same stanza or in the next stanza. We call this a 'run-on' line or **enjambement** – but understand the *effect* rather than remember the term! This technique gives the poet the freedom to start and end lines where he/she pleases – to give maximum emphasis to important words and phrases. Enjambement also tends to increase the pace of the poem compared to the pauses created by full stops at the ends of lines. You can hear this particularly when reading a poem containing enjambement out loud.

Key terms

Enjambement: 'overlapping' of a sentence onto a following line.

Prose: any piece of writing that is not in verse form.

Verse: another word for poetry.

Activity

3 If you look at the last two stanzas of 'The Pond', you will see that they are, in fact, one long sentence that could have been set out differently. The main effect of the poet's line organisation here is that 'vowing' and 'slink back' are given prominence. What effect does this have?

D. Prose into verse

As you have seen, poets think carefully about:

- which words to use
- where they should place their chosen words.

Below are the words of Imtiaz Dharker's poem 'Living Space', in which she describes her impressions of buildings in a shanty town in a developing country. They are written in **prose** form. You are going to experiment with different ways of placing these words into lines of **verse**.

There are just not enough straight lines. That is the problem. Nothing is flat or parallel. Beams balance crookedly on supports thrust off the vertical. Nails clutch at open seams. The whole structure leans dangerously towards the miraculous. Into this rough frame, someone has squeezed a living space and even dared to place these eggs in a wire basket, fragile curves of white hung out over the dark edge of a slanted universe, gathering the light into themselves, as if they were the bright, thin walls of faith.

Activities

1 Experiment with free verse form by organising the sentences of 'Living Space' into a poem. Read the sentences carefully before you do this. Remember what you have been taught about the effective placement of words and use of 'run-on' lines. You will need to make decisions about where to start new lines in order to:

- give the poem an appropriate shape that reflects what you think the meaning of the poem is

- emphasise important words and ideas that communicate the meaning of the poem.

Once you have done this, compare your version with a partner's and discuss why you decided to start and end the lines where you did.

2 Now study the original version of Imtiaz Dharker's poem on page 56. How close were you to the original word and line placement?

a With a partner, discuss the meaning of the poem. Which ideas and images in the poem are particularly important to the meaning?

b How are these ideas and images emphasised by the way they are arranged?

3 You have learned that free verse does not have a regular rhyme-scheme. What effect does a lack of a rhyme-scheme have on 'Living Space'? How do you think this helps to enhance the meaning of the poem?

Check your learning

You have learned in this chapter that a poet's placement of words can reinforce meaning. Read the following sentence, set out as prose: 'A butterfly goes up the barley rows, stitching together.' Now read the following haiku poem, by Japanese poet Sorab, which creates a clear image.

The Barleyfield

Up the barley rows,
Stitching, stitching together,
A butterfly goes.

The prose and the poem say the same thing. Write an explanation of why the poet has:

- chosen to repeat one of the words

- placed the words in a different order.

Background

A haiku is a short poem of three lines and 17 syllables, divided five, seven, five. It is a traditional Japanese form of poetry and often deals with images of nature.

6

Objectives

In this chapter you will:

learn what 'comparing' poems means

practise identifying similarities and differences between poems.

Comparing poems

In this chapter you are going to explore how to compare two unseen poems. The two poems you are going to explore are about similar topics. This will help you to focus your thinking and look more closely at important details.

You may or may not have to compare two poems in the unseen question on the exam paper you sit. However, even if you do not need to, it is probable that you will be asked to compare poems in another part of the exam based on set texts that you have studied with your teacher.

This chapter covers an approach to comparison that can be used whenever you need to compare poems in an exam response.

A. What comparison means

Comparison simply involves saying what similarities and differences you can see in poems in terms of content/ideas and style. These relate to the assessment criteria AO1 and AO2 that you will now be familiar with (see page 2).

It is likely that the subject matter of the two poems will have similarities, but the poems' situations, the poets' attitudes, and their approaches and styles, might be very different. For instance, you might be asked to write about two poems on the theme of parent/child relationships: such as a poem about childbirth from the point of view of a mother, compared with a poem about a bereaved father who has lost his son in war.

There are a number of aspects of poems that you might compare:
- content, themes, ideas
- setting
- atmosphere
- tone
- use of language and techniques (style)
- structure
- verse form.

In other words, you will be writing about the features of poetry you have studied in the previous chapters. You might like to 'skim' the contents of Chapters 1–5 in order to remind yourself of how some of the features listed above were explored.

Exam tip

Remember that comparing poems means looking for differences between poems, as well as similarities.

Throughout this book you have:

- practised annotation
- studied 'models' of brief notes on small amounts of text
- made your own notes on extracts.

You are going to use the annotation techniques again to help you focus on key similarities and differences between texts.

B. Focusing on what is important

Examiners often say that students underachieve by writing too much. They try to cover everything in a text but, because of this, they fail to analyse significant details in depth. It is important for you to demonstrate your skills in analysis. You need to show that you can think about, comment on and explore important aspects and details of a poem.

You do not have time in an exam to write about everything in a poem. It is better to write a lot about a limited amount of text than to write a little about a lot of text, because some sections of poems will be more significant than others and offer scope for more detailed comment.

You will understand why this is so if you think back to Chapter 4, where you studied the structure of the poem 'Street Gang'. You learned that a poem is often deliberately built up to a climax, so that the reader is left thinking about a key thought or 'message' that is expressed at the end of the poem. In this case, the poet asks the reader to think about the causes and implications of the senseless act of violence he has described earlier. It follows that if you made these closing lines a focus for your answer, you would succeed in dealing with important aspects of the writer's intentions.

Exam tip

You will gain more marks if you comment on important aspects of poems than if you simply describe their general features.

C. Getting to the heart of poems

The purpose of the following activities is to encourage you to:

- focus on key details in poems that help you to identify the writers' intentions and techniques
- use these selected details to think about similarities and differences between poems
- (later) practise using the details as a 'springboard' for a comparative essay.

In pairs, read 'Circus Lion' by C. Day-Lewis.

Circus Lion

Lumbering haunches, pussyfoot tread, a pride of
Lions under the arcs
Walk in, leap up, sit pedestalled there and glum
As a row of Dickensian clerks.

Their eyes are slag. Only a muscle flickering,
A bored, theatrical roar
Witness now to the furnaces that drove them
Exultant along the spoor.

In preyward, elastic leap they are sent through paper
Hoops at another's will
And a whip's crack: afterwards, in their cages,
They tear the provided kill.

Caught young, can this public animal ever dream of
Stars, distances and thunders?
Does he twitch in sleep for ticks, dried water-holes,
Rogue elephants, or hunters?

Sawdust, not burning desert is the ground
Of his to-fro, to-fro pacing,
Barred with the zebra shadows that imply
Sun's free wheel, man's coercing.

See this abdicated beast, once king
Of them all, nibble his claws:
Not anger enough left – no, nor despair –
To break his teeth on the bars.

Activities

1 Spend 5–10 minutes exchanging ideas with a partner on what you think the poem is about and discussing any interesting features of expression that you think help to convey the poet's ideas. Explain your interpretations, referring to details in the text.

2 On a piece of A4 paper, write in the centre the lines below and, with a partner, create a spider diagram of thoughts and ideas suggested by the words and how they are presented, adding to the example started for you:

If you 'abdicate', don't you <u>choose</u> to stand down?

See this abdicated beast, once king
Of them all, nibble his claws:

'king' stands out at end of line

3 Exchange your spider diagram with that of another pair and talk about similarities and differences in your ideas.

Now read 'The Jaguar' by Ted Hughes.

The Jaguar

The apes yawn and adore their fleas in the sun.
The parrots shriek as if they were on fire, or strut
Like cheap tarts to attract the stroller with the nut.
Fatigued with indolence, tiger and lion

Lie still as the sun. The boa-constrictor's coil
Is a fossil. Cage after cage seems empty, or
Stinks of sleepers from the breathing straw.
It might be painted on a nursery wall.

But who runs like the rest past these arrives
At a cage where the crowd stands, stares, mesmerized,
As a child at a dream, at a jaguar hurrying enraged
Through prison darkness after the drills of his eyes

On a short fierce fuse. Not in boredom –
The eye satisfied to be blind in fire,
By the bang of blood in the brain deaf the ear –
He spins from the bars, but there's no cage to him

More than to the visionary his cell:
His stride is wildernesses of freedom:
The world rolls under the long thrust of his heel.
Over the cage floor the horizons come.

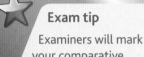

Activities

4 Repeat the process of Activities 1–3 on another piece of paper, in this poem focusing on:

> He spins from the bars, but there's no cage to him
>
> More than to the visionary his cell:

5 With your partner, go back to your notes on 'Circus Lion' and circle what seems to you the one word or phrase you have noted that seems the most important in showing what the poem is about. Now talk about how this word or phrase relates to the notes you have made on 'The Jaguar'. What similarities and differences can you see?

6 With your partner, quickly circle and annotate important details in the two whole poems. (Your teacher will give you copies to work on.)

7 Now study the annotated copies on pages 58–59 and compare your selections and ideas with those presented.

Exam tip

Examiners will mark your comparative work against the specific assessment criteria of AO3.

D. Making more detailed links

Now try to organise your ideas into clearer categories. Think carefully about the following aspects of the poems:

- the attitudes and ideas presented
- the language and imagery used
- the structure and form of the poems.

Creating and completing a table like the one shown below can help you to focus your thoughts and to plan what you will write. Copy the table and add to the ideas that are given.

Aspects	Poem 1: 'Circus Lion'	Poem 2: 'The Jaguar'
Attitudes and ideas *What is the poem about? What ideas is the poet exploring?*	Poet thinks animals have lost vitality and majesty.	Poet admires unchained energy – not like other creatures.
Language and imagery *What feelings are suggested by the words the poet has used?*	Athletic ('elastic leap'), but acting ('theatrical').	Lots of energetic verbs to suggest power – 'spins', 'hurrying enraged'.
Structure and form *How has the poet organised the lines of the poem and how does this affect your interpretation?*	Contrasts captivity with life in the wild (poem goes from present to past).	Contrasts jaguar with submissive creatures and increases pace dramatically after stanza 2.

Activity

1 If you had to write an essay comparing the two poems, the first thing you would need to do would be to establish what the main similarities and differences in the poets' approaches to the subject are. A possible essay title might be: 'Compare what the poets are saying about animals in captivity, and compare how they present their thoughts and feelings in the poems.'

Write your own introductory paragraph to this essay.

The following banks of words might be useful to help you write the paragraph or complete the essay.

Showing similarity:

- similarly
- also
- equally
- in the same way
- likewise
- both/each

Showing difference:

- on the other hand
- in contrast
- however
- instead
- whereas
- difference

You can draw on these throughout your response; they will help you to keep a clear focus on comparison.

Your paragraph might sound something like the following, which has been written about two imaginary poems (not the ones you are studying). Think about the wording of the example, but don't just try to copy – think for yourself!

Both the poems describe relationships between parents and children. However, 'poem X' is written in the first person from the point of view of a mother who has lost her young son in a car accident, whereas 'poem Y' is written in the third person about a grown-up woman searching for the identity of her father, who left home when she was a child. 'Poem X' uses lots of emotive language to convey the grief of the mother, as the accident has only just taken place; in contrast, the woman in 'poem Y' is going about her research calmly. Nevertheless, as she finds photographs of her father in an album never shown to her before by her mother, her heart skips a beat … Each poem uses contrast to …

Check your learning

In this chapter you have:

- learned what 'comparison' means and involves
- learned that concise essays that *comment* on ideas are better than long ones that merely *describe* content
- practised selecting and thinking about key details in poems.

In this section you will have to:

respond to texts critically and imaginatively; select and evaluate relevant detail to illustrate and support interpretations (AO1)

explain how language, structure and form contribute to writers' presentation of ideas, themes and settings (AO2)

for some examination boards you will also have to make comparisons and explain links between texts, evaluating writers' different ways of expressing meaning and achieving effects (AO3).

Exam tip

You do not have to write about features of poems in equal measure, so *develop* your ideas on aspects you consider especially important.

Exam practice

Introduction

This section of the book will enable you to apply the skills you have learned so far and to prepare specifically for your unseen poetry exam question. In the exam you will be given a poem that you have never seen before and must answer a question on it in essay form. You may be asked to analyse one unseen poem or you may be asked to compare two unseen poems. Either way, this section will help you to think about how you could respond to the exam question in the most effective way.

How you can prepare for the exam

You may find it helpful to remind yourself of the key aspects of poetry analysis you have covered in this book so far, before moving on to the exam practice in this section. You have explored in turn:

- a poem's themes and ideas
- the language used in a poem and its effects
- the imagery used in a poem and its effects
- the structure of a poem and how this contributes to its meaning
- the form of a poem and how this contributes to its meaning
- how two poems may be compared.

You will be using your learning to apply these skills in the following chapters, where you will examine sample exam questions, sample student responses and examiner commentaries.

You will only need to answer the question for the tier that you have been entered for in the exam. If you are entered for Foundation tier, your question may be broken down into parts or you may be provided with guiding bullet points. As in any exam, you should take time to read the question and think about what it is asking you to do. Read the poem(s) you are given carefully and do not rush straight into writing; think first about the key points you want to explore that will help you to answer the question effectively. Remember the Assessment Objectives that you will be marked against: AO1, AO2 and, if you are asked to compare two unseen poems, AO3. The paper that the unseen question appears in may also contain questions on other parts of your Literature course, so you must try to keep to the times suggested for each question so that you do not waste valuable time in the exam.

Using this section

This section is divided into three chapters. Chapter 7 offers guidance on how you could tackle one unseen poem in the exam. Chapter 8 offers guidance on how you could approach comparing two unseen poems in the exam. Both chapters present a sample exam-style question, with a sample student response and examiner commentary. You will also find that more sample questions are provided at the end of the chapters for you to practise applying your poetry analysis skills further.

These practice opportunities will help you to:

- ask the right sorts of questions about the poem(s)
- become more selective in the detail you choose to write about
- develop confidence in your ability to write about poetry.

Only one of these chapters will relate directly to what you need to do in an exam. This will depend on which exam board you are following. However, both chapters will help you to develop your skills in responding to poetry.

Finally, at the end of the book (pages 57–60), you will find some sample annotations of the poems used.

If you work through this section carefully, seeking guidance from your teacher when you need to, you will be better prepared for your exam. Good luck!

Exam tip

Make the most of practice opportunities; they will help you to become a more confident reader of unseen poetry.

7

Objectives

In this chapter you will:

learn about what is required of you in the unseen exam

apply and practise your skills in order to respond to the exam question effectively.

Making your skills count in the exam: analysing one unseen poem

About the exam

Structure and content of the exam

This book caters for students sitting exams with different exam boards, most of which have two tiers of paper, Higher and Foundation. Therefore, there will be two different questions, one for each tier, based on a given poem that you will not have seen before (unless you are lucky!). You must choose only the question for the tier your teacher has entered you for.

Mark schemes and styles of question differ from one exam board to another. In this chapter, a question similar to the style used by one chosen exam board is used, but in the practice questions suggested at the end of the chapter, you will find examples of questions that use different wording and formats. You need not worry about this. Shortly before the exam, your teacher will prepare you more specifically by:

- explaining what style of question you are likely to face and what the wording means
- explaining the mark scheme to you so that you know how to use your time in the exam, which is very important.

How you can prepare for the exam

Obviously, if you have not seen the poem before, you cannot revise for this question in the normal way. The preparation and practice you have had during the two years of the course will enable you to answer the question with confidence. You can, however, 'skim' through the first six chapters of this book and remind yourself of the key aspects of poetry they have covered. As 'last-minute' preparation, you could go back to the checklist in the introductory section to the 'unseen' chapters (page 3) and remind yourself of what to look for in a poem.

An effective practical way to revise might be to work with a partner, choosing poems from a poetry collection, such as old or current anthologies used by exam boards for set text study, and practise some of the types of reading activities you have come across while working through the chapters of Section B. Your teacher will advise you on suitable poems to choose.

You could:

- set each other questions on a poem and discuss 'answers'
- write statements about a poem and discuss why you think they are true
- highlight key words and phrases and ask your partner to comment on why they are effective
- both annotate a poem and compare notes.

Exam tip

Remember that there are no 'right' answers or fixed meanings in examiners' minds. What matters is that you are able to support your interpretations with evidence from the poem.

Chapter 7
Making your skills count in the exam:
analysing one unseen poem

What you need to know

Introducing the questions

Later on in this chapter you will find a sample essay by a student in response to the poem 'Coming Home' by Owen Sheers.

Whether you are taking the Foundation or Higher tier, the examiner will assess your answer(s) using the same assessment criteria, which cover the two Assessment Objectives you will by now be familiar with:

- AO1: respond to texts critically and imaginatively; select and evaluate relevant detail to illustrate and support interpretations.
- AO2: explain how language, structure and form contribute to writers' presentation of ideas, themes and settings.

Different exam boards will phrase the questions you will answer differently, so your exam question may look slightly different from the same question that follows, but it is really the *style* of questions that differs, not the *content*.

The sample question on 'Coming Home' on page 46 has been set as an example of a Foundation tier question. A Higher tier question might have been worded slightly differently but would be testing the same skills – those described in the Assessment Objectives given above.

Part (a) of the question asks: <u>What</u> do you think that <u>the poet is saying</u> about <u>the speaker's experience</u> in the poem?

A part of the question will always be about *content*. This is not just what the poem is about in terms of what happens in it, or what it describes, but what the poet's ideas, thoughts and attitudes are.

Part (b) of the question asks: <u>How</u> does the poet present the speaker's <u>attitudes</u> and <u>feelings</u> towards the experience?

The other part of the question will always be about the poet's *methods* and *techniques*: how they use language, structure and form to communicate ideas and descriptions effectively. Remember to comment on the *effect* of the techniques used. It is particularly in this part of the question that you will have to refer to details from the poem to support your ideas.

It is very important that you do not rush into writing before you have understood the poem. Spend at least five minutes reading and underlining important details you are likely to write about.

Exam tip

You will never have to break down the meaning of every line in a poem, so make sure that you do not waste valuable time doing this.

Exam tip

You will gain higher marks if you explain the effects of the poet's techniques rather than simply listing them.

You have 30 minutes to answer the questions printed at the end of the poem.

Coming Home

My mother's hug is awkward,
as if the space between her open arms
is reserved for a child, not this body of a man.
In the kitchen she kneads the dough,
flipping it and patting before laying in again.
The flour makes her over, dusting
the hairs on her cheek, smoothing out wrinkles.

*

Dad still goes and soaks himself in the rain.
Up to his elbows in hedge, he works
on a hole that reappears every Winter,
its edges laced with wet wool –
frozen breaths snagged on the blackthorn.
When he comes in again his hair is wild,
and his pockets are filled with filings of hay.

*

All seated, my grandfather pours the wine.
His unsteady hand makes the neck of the bottle
shiver on the lips of each glass;
it is a tune he plays faster each year.

(a) What do you think that the poet is saying about the speaker's experience in the poem?

(b) How does the poet present the speaker's attitudes and feelings towards the experience?

Getting to grips with the poem

Now work through the following activities to help you respond to the questions.

Activities

1 On a copy of the poem printed from the online resources, spend five minutes underlining key words and phrases you think you will need to write about in order to answer the questions.

2 Swap copies with a partner and spend ten minutes discussing what your chosen details mean and why they are important.

3 Now read and discuss the suggested annotations on the poem 'Coming Home' on page 57.

4 In exam conditions, spend 30 minutes answering the questions. Cover up the sample answer on the following page so that it does not distract you from thinking for yourself.

5 Read the sample answer and the examiner's commentary that follows.

Chapter 7
Making your skills count in the exam:
analysing one unseen poem

Sample answer

The following answer was written by Luke, a Year 11 student practising for the exam.

(a) The poem is about a man returning home after being away for a while. There is an awkwardness between him and his mother as though she does not know how to react to her grown-up son: 'My mother's hug is awkward … is reserved for a child'. When his mother is kneading the dough, the flour is on her face 'smoothing out wrinkles', which shows that the speaker has noticed how his mother has aged, which creates an unhappy atmosphere.

The speaker comments on how 'Dad still goes', which shows how his dad <u>still</u> does old habits, which could either be a happy moment making him feel more at home, or be a sad moment as if nothing about his family has changed.

The speaker's grandfather has 'unsteady hands', which shows how old he has become. This creates a depressing atmosphere.

The poet is saying that the speaker's experience is awkward and unhappy because his mother does not know how to react to him, and his family have all aged.

(b) The poet shows the speaker's thoughts and feelings by being very descriptive about his family's actions and appearances, this shows us what he is noticing about them.

The speaker notices his mother 'smoothing out wrinkles', telling us he realises that she is older now, showing us he is thinking about her appearance.

The poet writes 'Dad still goes', showing that the speaker is unhappy at how his family still have old habits.

The poet makes out that the speaker is worried about his grandfather because his 'unsteady hand' shakes on the wine bottle that hits the glasses as he pours wine, which is 'a tune he plays faster each year', telling us his grandfather grows more shaky and unsteady every year.

As stated earlier, it is not possible to write about every relevant detail in a poem in 30 minutes. The following commentary is designed to indicate some of the other points that might have gained the student more marks.

Answer to part (a)

Examiner's comment

This is a concise and focused answer. The student interprets the speaker's attitudes and feelings towards each of the three members of the family effectively, carefully selecting relevant quotations to explain and support his points. When writing about the father he offers alternative interpretations of the poet's intentions, which shows he is thinking flexibly.

The student has dealt with the content of the poem very thoroughly. However, it would also have been possible to point out that:

- although the speaker's feelings are never stated openly, he probably admires the fact that his parents are so hard-working and is comforted by the recognition of their domestic routines. He might also think they deserve more of a rest at their age, or might understand that their busy routine is what 'keeps them going'.

- the speaker never uses 'I' in the poem, which perhaps explains why the student thought the speaker to be a bit detached from the situation.

Answer to part (b)

Examiner's comment

The answer to part (b) is not as strong as the writing on part (a), but the student nevertheless interprets the effects of textual details quite well, especially the implications of the description of the grandfather's behaviour in the last stanza.

To improve his overall mark, the student might have:

- commented in more detail on how, in using verbs and onomatopoeic words to describe the mother, the poet helps us to visualise the scene. The last two lines of stanza 1 suggest that the speaker can briefly see his mother as the younger person she once was, because the flour hides her wrinkles.

- explained how the poet highlights his father's persistence in uncomfortable conditions ('Up to his elbows'). Sense impressions are important in the poem, for example 'frozen breaths snagged'.

- pointed out that the structure of the poem is simple: it focuses on the three family members in three distinct stanzas, separated by asterisks, which almost create 'islands'. Significantly, the last stanza is shorter, as if implying the grandfather does not have so long to live.

- explained that the free verse form helps to emphasise some words placed at the openings of lines. The last stanza is especially effective: 'His unsteady hand' and 'shiver' are prominently placed to stress his frailty. The semicolon before the final ominous line creates a dramatic pause.

Chapter 7
Making your skills count in the exam:
analysing one unseen poem

Practice exam questions

Your teacher will set you specific exam practice questions on appropriate poems, and guide you if you wish to choose poems for extra practice. All questions test your skills in meeting the Assessment Objectives AO1 and AO2, but the form of words is different for different exam boards and may even differ slightly from year to year, depending on the subject of the poem. Although you could choose the poems below to practise your skills, they are primarily included to show you how approaches to question-setting can differ.

You will see from the text below that you are more likely to be given bullet points to guide you if you are answering a Foundation tier question.

Foundation tier

1 Read Vernon Scannell's poem 'Autobiographical Note' and answer the questions that follow.

   (a) What do you think the poet is saying about the children's behaviour?

   (b) How does the poet make his description of the children's behaviour effective?

2. Read Alice Walker's 'Poem at Thirty-nine' and answer the following question.

   How does the poet explore the daughter's thoughts and feelings about her relationship with her father?

   Write about:

   ■ the impression the reader is given of the father
   ■ how the poet uses voice
   ■ how the poet has organised the poem in order to convey the daughter's feelings powerfully.

3. Read Gillian Clarke's 'On the Train' and answer the question that follows.

   What do you find particularly moving about this poem?

   You should consider:

   ■ the poet's situation – where the poet is and what she is doing
   ■ the situation of the person she is speaking to and her feelings about him
   ■ the words and phrases used by the poet to make the poem moving.

Higher tier

1. Read Philip Larkin's poem 'Toads' and answer the following question:

   Write about the poem 'Toads'.

   You should write about the poem and how the poet uses language to communicate his thoughts and feelings vividly.

2. Read Stephen Spender's poem 'The Pylons' and answer the question that follows:

   How does Stephen Spender present his ideas about the pylons. Support your answer (i.e. back up your ideas) with examples from the poem.

3. Read Ted Hughes' poem 'Thistles' and answer the following question. What do you think the poet is saying about the natural world and how does he make the description of the thistles vivid to the reader?

Check your learning

In this chapter you have:

● learned how to approach the unseen poetry exam
● practised your skills and considered how your response can be improved.

Objectives

Exam tip

Even if you are following a course that requires you to write about *one* unseen poem, the skills you practise in this chapter are still applicable to other parts of your course.

Making your skills count in the exam: comparing two unseen poems

About the exam

Structure and content of the exam

All GCSE English Literature students are required to compare texts. This may be covered in:

- Examination questions on set texts (usually poems from a prescribed anthology)
- An 'unseen' poetry comparative question.

While this section of the book is specifically for students doing the unseen poetry exam question, it will also support you if you are answering comparative questions on set anthology poems.

How you can prepare for the exam

The advice given in Chapter 7 (see page 44) on preparing to write about one unseen poem in an exam is just as relevant here, except that you will need to practise making notes on pairs of poems rather than single poems. In this case, you will probably need direction from your teacher about which linked poems to use.

What you need to know

Introducing the questions

Later in this chapter you will find a sample essay in response to a comparative question on Seamus Heaney's 'Honeymoon Flight' and 'Scaffolding'. (Usually the two poems will be by different poets.)

The examiner will assess your answer using *three* Assessment Objectives, as opposed to the two described in the previous chapter.

- AO1: respond to texts critically and imaginatively; select and evaluate relevant detail to illustrate and support interpretations.
- AO2: explain how language, structure and form contribute to writers' interpretations of ideas, themes and settings.
- AO3: make comparisons and explain links between texts, evaluating writers' different ways of expressing meaning and achieving effects.

The sample question reads as follows:

> Write about both poems and their effects on you. Show how they are similar and how they are different.

Chapter 8
Making your skills count in the exam:
comparing two unseen poems

Sometimes you will be given some brief background information about the poems, and sometimes explanations of difficult vocabulary. Usually you will be given some bullet points to help you direct your answer, such as the following:

You may wish to include some or all of these points:

- the content of the poems – what they are about
- the ideas the poet may have wanted us to think about
- the mood or atmosphere of the poems
- how they are written – words and phrases you find interesting, the way they are organised
- your responses to the poems.

As explained in the 'What you need to know' section in Chapter 7, you are basically being asked to comment on what the poems are about in terms of:

- situation, events and ideas
- how the poets use language and poetic techniques to communicate the content effectively.

To meet AO3, however, you will also need to comment on *what aspects of content and style are similar and what aspects are different*. The poems set will have a common topic or theme, but the poets' approaches and style may be quite different.

You will also be advised that 'You may write about each poem separately and then compare them, or make comparisons where appropriate in your answer as a whole'.

If you 'flit' from one poem to the other, your answer might lose focus, so perhaps the best method would be to:

- write a few introductory sentences saying what the poems seem to have in common
- write about one poem
- write about the other poem using *cross-references*, that is pointing out any similarities to and differences from the first poem as you go along
- write a few concluding sentences about important differences, without repeating points already made.

Exam tip

Remember that you will be marked against AO3 as well as AO1 and AO2 if you have to compare two unseen poems.

Sample question

In an exam you would have one hour to answer the question printed at the end of the two poems. The thinking and preparation you do before writing will help you produce a good answer.

Seamus Heaney is an Irish poet who has won the Nobel Prize for Literature. In the following poems he writes about love relationships at different stages in life.

Honeymoon Flight

Below, the patchwork earth, dark hems of hedge,
The long grey tapes of road that bind and loose
Villages and fields in casual marriage:
We bank above the small lough and farmhouse

And the sure green world goes topsy-turvy
As we climb out of our familiar landscape.
The engine noises change. You look at me.
The coastline slips away beneath the wing-tip.

And launched right off the earth by force of fire
We hang, miraculous, above the water,
Dependent on the invisible air
To keep us airborne and to bring us further.

Ahead of us the sky's a geyser now.
A calm voice talks of cloud yet we feel lost.
Air-pockets jolt our fears and down we go.
Travellers, at this point, can only trust.

Scaffolding

Masons, when they start upon a building,
Are careful to test out the scaffolding;

Make sure that planks won't slip at busy points,
Secure all ladders, tighten bolted joints.

And yet all this comes down when the job's done
Showing off walls of sure and solid stone.

So if, my dear, there sometimes seem to be
Old bridges breaking between you and me

Never fear. We may let the scaffolds fall
Confident that we have built our wall.

Key terms

Lough: lake (like the Scottish 'loch').

Mason: a person skilled in making things out of stone.

Write about both poems and their effects on you. Show how they are similar and how they are different.

Getting to grips with the poems

Now work through the following activities to help you respond to the questions. (Before you begin the activities, you might like to go back to Chapter 3 and remind yourself of what you learned about images from your study of 'The Thickness of Ice'.)

Chapter 8
Making your skills count in the exam:
comparing two unseen poems

Activities

1 On copies of poems provided by your teacher, spend ten minutes underlining key words and phrases you think you will need to write about in order to answer the question.

2 Swap copies with a partner and spend ten minutes discussing what your chosen details mean and why they are important.

3 Now read and discuss the suggested annotations on page 60.

4 Read the sample answer that follows and the examiner's commentary. Cover up the sample answer below so that it does not distract you from thinking for yourself.

Sample answer

The two poems are a bit puzzling at first until you realise that they are both about love and relationships. The plane journey and the building of a house represent the development of relationships, but in the first poem a relationship is beginning, and in the second the relationship is well established.

In the first poem, the speaker is describing his/her feelings about a new relationship as the couple fly off on honeymoon. The first stanza 'sets the scene' by giving a vivid visual impression of the land seen from the plane as it rises. The fields look like a 'patchwork' quilt with the hedges like 'dark hems' and the roads like 'long grey tapes' binding them together. The use of the word 'marriage' to describe the linking of parts of the landscape is interesting as the couple are also joined in marriage.

As the plane rises, and the coastline disappears, the speaker feels less secure. The ground was a 'sure green world', but now everything is 'topsy-turvy'. When he (I'll imagine it's a man from here) talks about 'the familiar landscape' they left behind, you could interpret this as representing the familiarity of his life before marriage, which is a new venture.

This idea is developed in the next stanza. 'Launched right off the earth by force of fire' refers to the engines, but also the passion that launched their relationship. However, there's only the 'invisible air' to take them forward, literally on the journey, but also on the journey of their future life, and air isn't very substantial!

In the last stanza, the poet contrasts the calmness of the pilot's voice as the plane goes into cloud with the couple's fear as they are jolted by the turbulence. Again, the air turbulence ('the sky's a geyser') probably also implies emotional turmoil. I like the way the poet builds up a picture of the speaker's thoughts and feelings using the extended comparison of the flight journey. The last line is a really effective climax. 'Travellers' have to go into unknown territory and trust they'll find their way, and so do the couple in the 'journey' of their relationship.

The second poem uses an extended comparison, too. The masons are like a couple building a relationship. They are wary at first and careful about the safety – or rather security – of their relationship. They are particularly careful at 'busy points' (times of pressure when the other person could get neglected?). Even strong points in the relationship are made more secure ('tighten bolted joints'), but when the building job's done (i.e. the relationship is 'cemented'), there's less need to be anxious about how they behave because trust has been established.

It's only in the fourth stanza with the reference to 'my dear' that the parallel between building and love becomes clear. In the last two stanzas, the poet uses the metaphor 'Old bridges breaking' to show how relationships change, but you don't have to worry if the relationship has good foundations. The last stanza emphasises the word 'Confident' to show that the couple don't need 'external' support (a 'scaffold') and can feel secure in their relationship.

I think 'security' sums up what the poems are about, but the speaker in the first poem is at the beginning of a relationship and doesn't feel secure, whereas the speaker in the second has an established relationship and is therefore more confident.

It isn't possible to include every relevant detail in a timed examination answer. The following commentary is intended to evaluate the quality of the essay and to suggest some of the other relevant points that might have been made.

Examiner's commentary

This is a very confident answer, in which the student shows excellent understanding of the poet's intentions in the two poems by analysing in detail the development of the two extended metaphors. He/she comments on the themes of the poems and the poet's methods concisely and thoughtfully, without feeling the need to use technical terms just for the sake of it. There is a strong individual response running through the essay (though an explanation of preference would have been interesting), and apt comparisons are made between the two poems, especially at the beginning and end of the answer. The student understands how the poet uses an extended comparison as a structure in both poems.

It would also have been possible to:

- Say more about the poet's approach and use of viewpoint in the two poems. In the first poem, Heaney uses description to create a particular setting that the reader can identify with, whereas the second poem is more abstract in its presentation of ideas. In the first poem the speaker describes his feelings and suggests they might be shared by his partner, whereas the speaker in the second poem addresses the partner to offer reassurance.

Chapter 8
Making your skills count in the exam:
comparing two unseen poems

- Examine the poet's deliberate word placement in particular sections of the poems. For instance, in the first poem, the word 'Dependent' is positioned at the opening of the line to emphasise a feeling of lack of control, and the use of commas around 'miraculous' and 'at this point' make the words stand out. In the first case, the speaker's awe at the special nature of his relationship is stressed, and in the second case, the phrase implies that confidence will develop as the relationship does (which has links with ideas in the second poem). The second poem is notable for its use of a series of strong statements designed to inspire confidence, with words and phrases such as 'Make sure', 'Secure', 'Never fear' and 'Confident' all being given particular prominence at the openings of lines.

Exam tip

Don't just generalise on the effects of a poet's use of language; comment on the effects of some specific examples of word choices and images.

Practice exam questions

If you wish to practise writing a comparative exam answer, ask your teacher to select a pair of poems, and use the question format introduced at the start of the chapter:

Write about both poems and their effects on you. Show how they are similar and how they are different.

As examples, some of the following pairs of poems could be used:
- 'Twice Shy' by Seamus Heaney and 'They Did Not Expect This' by Vernon Scannell
- 'Follower' by Seamus Heaney and 'Catrin' by Gillian Clarke
- 'Havisham' by Carol Ann Duffy and 'The Hunchback in the Park' by Dylan Thomas.

Check your learning

In this chapter you have:
- learned how to approach comparing two unseen poems in the exam
- applied your skills and considered how your response can be improved.

Appendix
Poem texts

The Face of Hunger

I counted the ribs on his concertina chest
bones protruding as if chiselled
by a sculptor's hand of famine.

He looked with glazed pupils
seeing only a bun on some sky-high shelf.

The skin was pale and taut
like a glove on a doctor's hand.

His tongue darted in and out
like a chameleon's
snatching a confetti of flies.

O! child,
your stomach is a den of lions
roaring day and night.

Living Space

There are just not enough
straight lines. That
is the problem.
Nothing is flat
or parallel. Beams
balance crookedly on supports
thrust off the vertical.
Nails clutch at open seams.
The whole structure leans dangerously
towards the miraculous.

Into this rough frame,
someone has squeezed
a living space

and even dared to place
these eggs in a wire basket,
fragile curves of white
hung out over the dark edge
of a slanted universe,
gathering the light
into themselves,
as if they were
the bright, thin walls of faith.

Disabled

He sat in a wheeled chair, waiting for dark,
And shivered in his ghastly suit of grey,
Legless, sewn short at elbow. Through the park
Voices of boys rang saddening like a hymn,
Voices of play and pleasure after day,
Till gathering sleep had mothered them from him.

         *   *   *

About this time Town used to swing so gay
When glow-lamps budded in the light blue trees,
And girls glanced lovelier as the air grew dim, –
In the old times, before he threw away his knees.
Now he will never feel again how slim
Girls' waists are, or how warm their subtle hands;
All of them touch him like some queer disease.

         *   *   *

There was an artist silly for his face,
For it was younger than his youth, last year.
Now, he is old; his back will never brace;
He's lost his colour very far from here,
Poured it down shell-holes till the veins ran dry,
And half his lifetime lapsed in the hot race,
And leap of purple spurted from his thigh.

         *   *   *

One time he liked a blood-smear down his leg,
After the matches, carried shoulder-high.
It was after football, when he'd drunk a peg,
He thought he'd better join. – He wonders why.
Someone had said he'd look a god in kilts,
That's why; and may be, too, to please his Meg;
Aye, that was it, to please the giddy jilts
He asked to join. He didn't have to beg;
Smiling they wrote his lie; aged nineteen years.
Germans he scarcely thought of; all their guilt,
And Austria's, did not move him. And no fears
Of Fear came yet. He thought of jewelled hilts
For daggers in plaid socks; of smart salutes;
And care of arms; and leave; and pay arrears;
Espirit de corps; and hints for young recruits.
And soon, he was drafted out with drums and cheers.

         *   *   *

Some cheered him home, but not as crowds cheer Goal.
Only a solemn man who brought him fruits
Thanked him; and then inquired about his soul.

         *   *   *

Now, he will spend a few sick years in Institutes,
And do what things the rules consider wise,
And take whatever pity they may dole.
To-night he noticed how the women's eyes
Passed from him to the strong men that were whole.
How cold and late it is! Why don't they come
And put him into bed? Why don't they come?

Analysing one unseen poem: sample annotation

The following is a sample annotation for the poem that appears in Chapter 7.

Coming Home

Self-conscious, coming to terms with his growing up. The poet never uses 'I' – seems a bit detached on the surface

My mother's hug is awkward,
as if the space between her open arms
is reserved for a child, not this body of a man.
In the kitchen she kneads the dough,
flipping it and patting before laying in again.
The flour makes her over, dusting
the hairs on her cheek, smoothing out wrinkles.

Always a place for him

These verbs create an energetic effect and 'flipping' and 'patting' are onomatopoeic

Made to look younger and more attractive

*

Dad still goes and soaks himself in the rain.
Up to his elbows in hedge, he works
on a hole that reappears every Winter,
its edges laced with wet wool –
frozen breaths snagged on the blackthorn.
When he comes in again his hair is wild,
and his pockets are filled with filings of hay.

Persistent and determined

Lots of sense impressions – these are details we can visualise

Simple structure – focuses on three separate people in different stanzas; separation is emphasised by asterisks. They are each 'islands' – each self-absorbed?

Would feel uncomfortable

*

All seated, my grandfather pours the wine.
His unsteady hand makes the neck of the bottle
shiver on the lips of each glass;
it is a tune he plays faster each year.

Emphatic line position

Climax: passage of time which leads to death; 'tune' here could be ironic

Dramatic pause

Comparing two unseen poems: sample annotations

The following are sample annotations for the poems that appear in Chapter 6 and Chapter 8.

Chapter 6

Circus Lion

Agile but muscular → Lumbering haunches, pussyfoot tread, a pride of
Lions under the arcs

Centre of attention but not happy → Walk in, leap up, sit pedestalled there and glum
As a row of Dickensian clerks.

Not alert → Their eyes are slag. Only a muscle flickering,
A bored, theatrical roar — Acting
Witness now to the furnaces that drove them — Old vitality
Exultant along the spoor.

Natural agility → In preyward, elastic leap they are sent through paper
Hoops at another's will ← Like slaves
And a whip's crack: afterwards, in their cages,
They tear the provided kill. — Lost hunting instincts

'Indoctrinated' → Caught young, can this public animal ever dream of
Stars, distances and thunders? ← Natural habitat
Does he twitch in sleep for ticks, dried water-holes,
Rogue elephants, or hunters? ← Rhetorical questions?

Confined and restless, contrast of environments → Sawdust, not burning desert is the ground
Of his to-fro, to-fro pacing,
Barred with the zebra shadows that imply
Contrast → Sun's free wheel, man's coercing.

See this abdicated beast, once king
Of them all, nibble his claws: — Trivial, not majestic
Given up → Not anger enough left – no, nor despair –
To break his teeth on the bars.

Points to consider:
- contrast – where lions are/where they should be
- key words emphasised at openings (especially) and at ends of lines
- monotonous rhythm?

The Jaguar

Boredom —→ The apes yawn and adore their fleas in the sun.

The parrots shriek as if they were on fire, or strut ←— Contrast with first line

Like cheap tarts to attract the stroller with the nut.

A contradiction? —→ Fatigued with indolence, tiger and lion

Lie still as the sun. The boa-constrictor's coil

Dead (but also visual likeness) —→ Is a fossil. Cage after cage seems empty, or ←— Monotonous

Stinks of sleepers from the breathing straw.

It might be painted on a nursery wall. ←— Short sentences and words with long vowel sounds make first 2 stanzas slow-paced

Signals change —→ But who runs like the rest past these arrives

At a cage where the crowd stands, stares, mesmerized,

As a child at a dream, at a jaguar hurrying enraged ←— Change of pace, little punctuation – protest?

Through prison darkness after the drills of his eyes ←—

Power —→ On a short fierce fuse. Not in boredom – ←— Not 'given in'

The eye satisfied to be blind in fire,

By the bang of blood in the brain deaf the ear –

He spins from the bars, but there's no cage to him ←— Thinks he's in the wild – imagination?

More than to the visionary his cell:

His stride is wildernesses of freedom:

Seems in control —→ The world rolls under the long thrust of his heel.

Over the cage floor the horizons come.

Points to consider:
- lots of sense impressions
- contrast between the jaguar and the other animals
- change of pace.

Chapter 8

Scene set by title → **Honeymoon Flight**

Below, the patchwork earth, dark hems of hedge, ← Visual details
The long grey tapes of road that bind and loose
Villages and fields in casual marriage; ← Joining
We bank above the small lough and farmhouse

Contrast between security and turmoil →
And the sure green world goes topsy-turvy
As we climb out of our familiar landscape. ← Old life before marriage
The engine noises change. You look at me.

Further away from safety of land →
The coastline slips away beneath the wing-tip.

And launched right off the earth by force of fire ← Passion
We hang, miraculous, above the water,
Dependent on the invisible air
Development of relationship → To keep us airborne and to bring us further.

Ahead of us the sky's a geyser now. ← Suggests emotional turmoil
Contrast with turmoil of 'geyser' → A calm voice talks of cloud yet we feel lost.
Air-pockets jolt our fears and down we go.
Journey through life → Travellers, at this point, can only trust. ← Key word to end poem

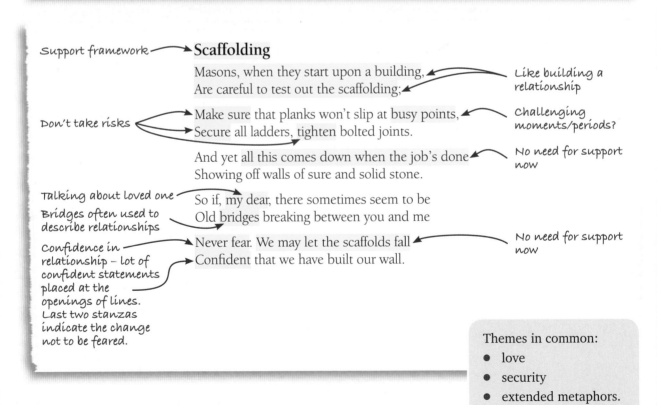

Support framework → **Scaffolding**

Masons, when they start upon a building, ← Like building a relationship
Are careful to test out the scaffolding;

Don't take risks → Make sure that planks won't slip at busy points, ← Challenging moments/periods?
Secure all ladders, tighten bolted joints.

And yet all this comes down when the job's done ← No need for support now
Showing off walls of sure and solid stone.

Talking about loved one → So if, my dear, there sometimes seem to be
Bridges often used to describe relationships → Old bridges breaking between you and me

Confidence in relationship – lot of confident statements placed at the openings of lines. Last two stanzas indicate the change not to be feared. →
Never fear. We may let the scaffolds fall ← No need for support now
Confident that we have built our wall.

Themes in common:
- love
- security
- extended metaphors.

60